D0471483

Our Best Friends

The Golden Retriever

Our Best Friends

The Boxer
Caring for Your Mutt
The German Shepherd
The Golden Retriever
The Labrador Retriever
The Poodle
The Shih Tzu
The Yorkshire Terrier

Our Best Friends

The Golden Retriever

September Morn

ELDORADO INK

Produced by OTTN Publishing, Stockton, New Jersey

Eldorado Ink
PO Box 100097
Pittsburgh, PA 15233
www.eldoradoink.com

Printed and bound in Malaysia.

First printing

1 3 5 7 9 8 6 4 2

Library of Congress Cataloging-in-Publication Data

Morn, September B.
The golden retriever / September Morn.
p. cm. — (Our best friends)
Includes bibliographical references and index.
ISBN-13: 978-1-932904-22-2 (hc)
ISBN-10: 1-932904-22-0 (hc)
1. Golden retriever—Juvenile literature. I. Title.
SF429.G63M67 2008
636.752'7—dc22

2007044877

Photo credits: Courtesy the Gerald Ford Presidential Library: 17; © Paula Holzapfel: 10, 49, 56, 72, front cover (left bottom); © iStockphoto/Rich Legg: 3, front cover (left center); © iStockphoto/Craig Smith: 74; © Jupiterimages: 27; © Michelle Lawlor: 94, 99; © Joel Mills: 75; courtesy the National Association of Professional Pet Sitters: 71; used under license from Shutterstock, Inc.: 8, 12, 15, 18, 20, 22, 23, 25, 28, 30, 32, 35, 36, 38, 40, 41, 44, 47, 48, 50, 54, 55, 58, 61, 62, 63, 65, 66, 67, 69, 78, 81, 82, 87, 89, 90, 92, 97, 100, front cover (main and left top), back cover.

TABLE OF CONTENTS

Introduction

GARY KORSGAARD, DVM

The mutually beneficial relationship between humans and animals began long before the dawn of recorded history. Archaeologists believe that humans began to capture and tame wild goats, sheep, and pigs more than 9,000 years ago. These animals were then bred for specific purposes, such as providing humans with a reliable source of food or providing furs and hides that could be used for clothing or the construction of dwellings.

Other animals had been sought for companionship and assistance even earlier. The dog, believed to be the first animal domesticated, began living and working with Stone Age humans in Europe more than 14,000 years ago. Some archaeologists believe that wild dogs and humans were drawn together because both hunted the same prey. By taming and training dogs, humans became more effective hunters. Dogs, meanwhile, enjoyed the social contact with humans and benefited from greater access to food and warm shelter. Dogs soon became beloved pets as well as trusted workers. This can be seen from the many artifacts depicting dogs that have been found at ancient sites in Asia, Europe, North America, and the Middle East.

The earliest domestic cats appeared in the Middle East about 5,000 years ago. Small wild cats were probably first attracted to human settlements because plenty of rodents could be found wherever harvested grain was stored. Cats played a useful role in hunting and killing these pests, and it is likely that grateful humans rewarded them for this assistance. Over time, these small cats gave up some of their aggressive wild behaviors and began living among humans. Cats eventually became so popular in ancient Egypt that they were believed to possess magical powers. Cat statues were placed outside homes to ward off evil spirits, and mummified cats were included in royal tombs to accompany their owners into the afterlife.

Today, few people believe that cats have supernatural powers, but most pet owners feel a magical bond with their pets, whether they are dogs, cats, hamsters, rabbits, horses, or parrots. The lives of pets and their people become inextricably intertwined, providing strong emotional and physical rewards for both humans and animals. People of all ages can benefit from the loving companionship of a pet. Not surprisingly, then, pet ownership is widespread. Recent statistics indicate that about 60 percent of all households in the United States and Canada have at least one pet, while the figure is close to 50 percent of households in the United Kingdom. For millions of people, therefore, pets truly have become their "best friends."

Finding the best animal friend can be a challenge, however. Not only are there many types of domesticated pets, but each has specific needs, characteristics, and personality traits. Even within a category of pets, such as dogs, different breeds will flourish in different surroundings and with different treatment. For example, a German Shepherd may not be the right pet for a person living in a cramped urban apartment; that person might be better off caring for a smaller dog like a Toy Poodle or Shih Tzu, or perhaps a cat. On the other hand, an active person who loves the outdoors may prefer the companionship of a Labrador Retriever to that of a small dog or a passive indoor pet like a goldfish or hamster.

The joys of pet ownership come with certain responsibilities. Bringing a pet into your home and your neighborhood obligates you to care for and train the pet properly. For example, a dog must be housebroken, taught to obey your commands, and trained to behave appropriately when he encounters other people or animals. Owners must also be mindful of their pet's particular nutritional and medical needs.

The purpose of the OUR BEST FRIENDS series is to provide a helpful and comprehensive introduction to pet ownership. Each book contains the basic information a prospective pet owner needs in order to choose the right pet for his or her situation and to care for that pet throughout the pet's lifetime. Training, socialization, proper nutrition, potential medical issues, and the legal responsibilities of pet ownership are thoroughly explained and discussed, and an abundance of expert tips and suggestions are offered. Whether it is a hamster, corn snake, guinea pig, or Labrador Retriever, the books in the OUR BEST FRIENDS series provide everything the reader needs to know about how to have a happy, well-adjusted, and well-behaved pet.

If you're looking for a friendly and enthusiastic canine pal, a Golden Retriever may be the perfect choice.

CHAPTER ONE

Is a Golden Retriever Right for You?

The Golden Retriever is an enthusiastic and willing worker and an intelligent, affectionate, and thoroughly charming animal companion. These versatile dogs, bred to retrieve on land and in water, are quick learners and can readily remember what they've been taught. Naturally gentle and patient with children, they make wonderful family dogs.

The Golden Retriever is powerful, muscular, alert, active, and agile, with a gentle disposition, a merrily wagging tail, and a ready-for-action attitude. Goldens are generally self-confident, stable, and sociable, and normally get along well with people, dogs, and other animals. The Golden Retriever is not a guard dog, but he can be an excellent watchdog. Friendly toward people in most situations, the Golden will bark a loud greeting when people arrive, though typically without aggressive overtones. This lets the owner know that someone is there, but doesn't intimidate legitimate visitors.

Golden Retrievers are easily trained using gentle methods and can learn many different skills. They can hunt ducks at dawn with Dad, fetch a ball with the kids after school, and then perform heartwarming tricks with Mom during an evening visit to a nursing home. A properly trained Golden Retriever will be polite and behave appropriately both at home and in public.

However, Goldens also have a well-developed sense of silliness and are likely to repeat naughty antics that make people laugh.

These dogs like to be active and are always eager for a good game. Goldens are fleet and agile on land, and they're usually strong swimmers. They enjoy accompanying their people wherever they go, and, if socialized properly when they're young, tend to make friends quickly with new dogs or humans. With all the Golden Retriever's exemplary characteristics, it's not surprising that this handsome and personable breed enjoys a steady position of popularity in the United States, Canada, Great Britain, and many other countries.

Golden Retrievers were bred as working dogs, so they enjoy opportunities to perform tasks and tricks.

Keep your Golden happy by giving him a job of his own. He'll happily carry your mail—as long as you don't mind a little drool on your letters!

Your Golden will be happiest if he feels useful and appreciated, so give him a few "jobs" to carry out each day, like fetching his own leash before walks or bringing his empty food dish to you when he finishes eating. Goldens will enthusiastically do whatever they've been trained to do, and having the opportunity to do your bidding will give your Golden Retriever a sense of accomplishment and pride.

A Golden Retriever with too much time on his paws will probably take up a hobby to keep from getting bored. Because they're retrievers by heritage, Golden Retrievers' self-taught hobbies usually have something to do with putting things into their mouths and carrying them around. Bored Goldens often engage in "counter surfing," seeking out and removing both food and nonfood items from counters and tables and then depositing them in other places, sometimes after a thorough chewing. A variation on that hobby is "collecting," which involves finding and carrying off certain preferred (and usually forbidden) items and depositing them all in one spot—often a spot humans might not readily notice. If sandwiches or spoons start disappearing from your kitchen counter or shoes in singles or pairs start disappearing from their proper place, you might reasonably suspect that your Golden Retriever has found a little hobby to pass the time.

The Golden Retriever's life expectancy is twelve to fourteen years.

To live happily with a Golden Retriever, train him in manners and obedience while he's growing and developing both physically and mentally. He will learn to be well behaved as a natural part of life. Also, provide him with daily physical and mental exercise, so he has appropriate outlets for his energy and intellect. If your lifestyle keeps you away from home for long days all week, and then on weekends you enjoy activities that don't involve dogs, you'll have trouble meeting a Golden Retriever's need for exercise and mental stimulation.

However, if you enjoy the steady, devoted companionship of an affectionate, intelligent, and handsome dog, and you're willing and able to provide the daily exercise and mental stimulation such a dog needs, a Golden Retriever may be a good choice for you. If you like to spend time with a very smart dog and you value a good-looking canine pal who applies himself enthusiastically to any job or trick you teach him, a Golden Retriever might be your perfect match. If you already have a Golden, you probably already know that this is the breed for you.

ROLES FOR YOUR GOLDEN RETRIEVER

Golden Retrievers make excellent pets and companion dogs for individuals or families because Goldens enjoy being with their special people and form bonds of deep love and loyalty. They serve admirably as guide dogs, hearing dogs, and assistance dogs for disabled individuals, and they can be very effective as emotional therapy dogs as well.

By nature and breeding, Golden Retrievers are hunting dogs, so if you enjoy that pastime your Golden will probably be delighted to accompany you. Not every Golden owner is a hunter, of course, but Goldens don't

Golden Retrievers love to be outdoors. These dogs were bred for hunting, but will be perfectly happy going on walks through the woods with their owners.

need to hunt to have a fulfilling life. Being a best buddy to you and your family will make your Golden Retriever happy and satisfied.

Beyond the joys of simple companionship, you and your Golden might discover that you enjoy competition sports like Agility, Obedience, Rally, Tracking, Flyball, Canine Musical Freestyle, Field Trials, and Conformation shows. The bond between dog and handler that develops through training and competing in dog sports and activities can greatly enhance your relationship with your Golden, as you learn to work together as a team. If you do a good job teaching your Golden Retriever what you want him to do, he'll try his best to excel in whatever role you need or want him to take.

BEST ENVIRONMENT FOR A GOLDEN RETRIEVER

Golden Retrievers were originally bred to hunt and retrieve birds and small game. The high work drive and natural desire to please that characterize a good retriever have remained strong in this breed. Goldens enjoy training sessions, thrive on learning new skills, and enjoy performing all the tasks, tricks, and duties they've been taught.

Golden Retrievers need to interact closely with their human family or special person. In any type of home environment, good training will help the Golden Retriever understand his owner's expectations and how to behave appropriately.

A Golden Retriever's natural hunting instincts can place him in danger if he follows a game trail or chases a bird or animal across a busy road.

You'll have to give your Golden plenty of exercise and opportunities to be active daily, with long walks and vigorous free exercise, like fetch games or swimming. After their daily workout, most Golden Retrievers are able to settle down comfortably and relax with the family.

The Golden Retriever is a versatile dog, both in the type of work he can do and the type of environment to which he can adapt. A Golden can be equally content in rural areas or cities, as long as he has proper exercise, a useful job or task to do, and a person he loves to do it for.

COSTS INVOLVED BEYOND THE PURCHASE PRICE

Regardless of whether you acquire your Golden Retriever for free or pay a king's ransom for him, that initial price is just the beginning of what your dog will cost over his lifetime. The price of maintaining a Golden Retriever will vary, depending on his age, his health, the cost of food and veterinary services, and the lifestyle you choose for him. Here's a list of the approximate basic expenses necessary to maintain a Golden Retriever for a year. Keep in mind that as the cost of living changes, so does the cost of owning a dog.

Food: $300 to $1,000, depending on what type of food you feed your Golden Retriever. Foods with better-quality ingredients typically cost more, but "cheap" dog food is often no bargain, because the better-quality foods are more nourishing, more palatable, easier to digest, and more beneficial to the dog's overall health.

Veterinary care: $200 to $500. These costs reflect the price of well-dog care, including veterinary exams, immunizations, and protection from heartworm, fleas, ticks, and other parasites. Illnesses, accidents, or injuries will quickly increase this expense by hundreds or thousands of dollars.

An active 80-pound (36-kg) adult Golden Retriever needs to eat approximately four cups (960 ml) of premium dry kibble food or two-and-a-half pounds (1 kg) of fresh meat and bone each day.

Training: $150 to $2,000. Training costs vary widely, depending on whether you take private or group lessons and what kind of training you're doing with your Golden. Basic manners classes are the bare minimum. To fully enjoy your Golden Retriever, continue training beyond the basic skills and develop your dog's inherent talents.

Grooming: $50 to $800, depending on whether you bathe and groom your Golden Retriever yourself or hire a groomer to perform these tasks. The high-end estimate is based on one professional grooming per month.

Everyday essentials: $150 to $600. This category includes such everyday items as collars, leashes, food dishes, chew toys, beds and bedding.

These basic costs add up to a minimum of $850 a year, but they could go much higher, depending on the cost of living in your area and how much your family wants to pamper your Golden Retriever.

CHAPTER TWO

Breed History and Background

In 1864, Dudley Marjoribanks, later known as Lord Tweedmouth, purchased a yellow male puppy, named Nous, from a cobbler near the town of Brighton in southern England. Nous was the only yellow pup in a litter of black, wavy-coated retrievers. The cobbler had received him, in payment of a debt, from the gamekeeper of Lord Chichester, a local landowner. Marjoribanks took Nous with him to his estate at

Golden Retrievers were developed by cross-breeding hunting dogs in Scotland.

Inverness-Shire, Scotland, as the newest addition to his kennel of sporting dogs.

One of Marjoribanks's hobbies was breeding hunting dogs, with the goal of developing a retriever particularly well suited to the climate, terrain, and game found in Scotland. In 1868 and 1871, Nous was bred to a Tweed Water Spaniel (a now-extinct breed) named Belle. These matings resulted in several yellow pups that formed the foundation stock for Marjoribanks's line of yellow retrievers.

The descendants of Nous and Belle were bred with wavy and flat-coated retrievers, another Tweed Water Spaniel, and a red setter. These yellow retrievers made good gamekeepers' dogs and hunting dogs, because Marjoribanks kept working ability foremost in his breeding plan. The descendants of these dogs became the breed we know today as the Golden Retriever.

Golden Retrievers first appeared at dog shows around 1906. Described initially as "Retriever—Wavy or Flat Coated," the breed was officially recognized in 1911, by the Kennel Club of the United Kingdom, as "Retriever—Yellow or Golden." In 1920 the Kennel Club of the United Kingdom changed the designation to "Retriever—Golden." The Golden Retriever was officially recognized as a breed and given show privileges by the Canadian Kennel Club in 1925 and by the American Kennel Club in 1932.

In 1932, Colonel Samuel Magoffin of Vancouver, British Columbia, imported from England a male Golden Retriever named Speedwell Pluto. This dog became a Canadian and American Conformation champion, and was the first Golden Retriever ever to win a Best in Show award. Speedwell Pluto was beautiful in the show ring and an excellent hunter, so he was highly valued as a stud dog in the United States and Canada. This dog is considered the foundation sire for the Golden Retriever breed in the United States.

Because of the breeders' original intentions, the Golden Retriever has always been an enthusiastic worker. The same traits of body and mind

In November 1925, Captain C. Waterhouse became the first person to register a Golden Retriever in the United States. That Golden's name was Lomberdale Blondin.

A GOLDEN IN THE WHITE HOUSE

Although Golden Retrievers have frequently participated at shows and field trials since their acceptance by the American Kennel Club in 1932, the breed was not well known to the American public until 1974. That fall the new president, Gerald Ford, acquired an eight-month-old female Golden Retriever puppy named Liberty. Later, when Liberty had a litter in the White House, it attracted a great deal of media attention. All of a sudden, the number of Golden Retriever registrations by the American Kennel Club soared. Today, the Golden Retriever is one of the top five most popular breeds in the United States.

that make the Golden such a great hunting partner also give him the ability to excel in guide dog and assistance dog work, search and rescue, Obedience and Tracking competitions, and many other activities that require focus, diligence, and persistence. With this breed's trainability, gentleness, and cooperative nature, the Golden Retriever has become one of the world's most popular breeds.

BREED STANDARDS AND CONFORMATION

Each purebred dog breed has a "parent club," which is organized and led by fanciers of that breed and experienced breeders. In the United States, the parent club of this breed is the Golden Retriever Club of America. In Great Britain, the parent club is the Golden Retriever Club of the United Kingdom, although there are smaller clubs covering Scotland,

Purebred Golden Retrievers are expected to exhibit certain physical characteristics, such as a squarish form and a thick double coat. The proper characteristics are described in the breed standard.

Wales, and various regions of England (such as Midland, Berkshire Downs, and Northumbria.) In Canada, the parent club is the Golden Retriever Club of Canada.

Each parent club develops a written description of the perfect dog of that breed; this is the standard by which dogs of that breed are judged in the show ring. Known as the Standard of Perfection, it is usually referred to simply as The Standard. This description of the breed always covers the proper appearance and gait, and many breed standards also include a description of the ideal temperament for this breed. Reputable breeders strive to produce dogs that conform to the Standard of Perfection as closely as possible.

Some breed standards are more detailed than others, but even a finely

A Golden Retriever with undershot or overshot jaws or a deviation in height of more than one inch (2.5 cm) above or below the heights called for in the breed standard is automatically disqualified from the Conformation ring.

detailed description leaves some room for individual interpretation. That's why Golden Retrievers from different breeding bloodlines can vary quite a bit in color and other aspects of their appearance.

APPEARANCE AND CHARACTERISTICS OF THE BREED

Golden Retrievers have a broad and slightly arched skull, a fairly long foreface, and a strong, deep muzzle, which is well suited for fetching and carrying game. The nose should be black or a blackish-brown, although the color may fade a little during the winter. The Golden Retriever's ears should be fringed with hair that is slightly longer than the rest of his coat. The ears should fall close to the cheek; if pulled forward, the tips of the ears should just cover the eyes.

A Golden Retriever's eyes should be brown, preferably a darker shade, with a friendly expression. Your Golden will express his emotions through his eyes. When he feels playful, his eyes will beam with mischief and delight. When he's happy, his eyes will light up with joy, and when he's sad, his eyes will reflect that, as well.

The Golden has a medium-length, water-repellent double coat. The dense outer coat may be straight or wavy. It should lie close to the body and will feel firm and resilient to the touch, rather than either coarse or silky. The undercoat is soft and dense, so it insulates the Golden Retriever against chilly winds and water. The coat is shorter on the head, paws, and the front of the legs, and has longer "feathering" on the chest, the back of the legs, under the body, and on the underside of the tail.

When the coat undergoes its twice-a-year shedding, these dogs drop huge amounts of fur, especially the fluffy undercoat. During this period your Golden will need a thorough brushing

Adult Golden Retrievers have 42 teeth; 20 in the upper jaw and 22 in the lower jaw.

every day, and your home will require daily sweeping or vacuuming.

The Golden's coat color can range from a pale gold to a deep red-gold, but a pure golden hue is preferable to extremely light or dark colors. Feathering on the legs and tail can be lighter than the rest of the coat. There should be no black markings on a Golden Retriever, and no white markings other than age-related graying and a few white hairs on the chest.

When fully grown, Golden Retrievers should weigh between 55 and 75 pounds (25 and 34 kg) and can measure between 20.5 and 25 inches (52 and 63.5 cm) tall at the withers (the highest point of the shoulders), though 21 to 24 inches (53.3 to 61 cm) is the preferred range. Males generally will fall into the upper half of the size and weight ranges; females will fall in the lower half. When viewed from the side, the Golden Retriever should present an outline that is almost square. His length from the front of his breastbone to the rear point of the buttocks

In judging the coat of a Golden Retriever, there is a wide range of acceptable shades of gold.

should be only slightly greater than his height at the withers. The ideal ratio of length to height is 12:11.

When a Golden Retriever walks, there is both lightness and determination in his stride. The Golden's trot is smooth and powerful, and when he gallops he can cover ground quickly. A Golden Retriever in good physical condition can work or play hard for hours before seeking a break. Sometimes a Golden can get so wrapped up in an athletic activity that he will overtire himself without seeming to notice. When playing or working with your Golden, make sure he gets rest breaks at appropriate intervals, so he can cool off and catch his breath.

Golden Retrievers are highly intelligent, affable, and energetic. They make wonderful pets and are excellent work partners for a variety of jobs. They seem to make friends naturally wherever they go. Goldens draw positive attention to themselves (and by association, to their owners) because of their lustrous golden coat, their warm and playful expression, and their upbeat and optimistic attitude.

Some of the famous people who have owned Golden Retrievers include Chevy Chase, Bob Newhart, Ed McMahon, Frank Gifford, Mary Tyler Moore, Bill Blass, Jimmy Stewart, Neil Diamond, and Oprah Winfrey.

CHAPTER THREE

Responsible Pet Ownership

As the owner of a Golden Retriever, you are morally responsible for his care and training. You are also legally responsible for any damage your dog might cause, and for knowing the laws governing dog ownership where you live.

Golden Retrievers are large dogs that need plenty of exercise. Your backyard should be a safe, fenced-in area in which your dog can play.

Each state, county, and municipality has its own set of rules that dog owners must obey. One type of rule almost every urban and suburban community enforces is the licensing of dogs.

Licensing costs vary considerably, but almost all communities charge less—often significantly less—to license a spayed or neutered dog than an intact one. Unlicensed dogs, if picked up as strays, usually earn their owners a steep fine for failing to comply with licensing laws, plus the cost of buying a license. That means you'll need to abide by all licensing requirements in your area, and you should make sure to properly identify your dog in case he gets lost or stolen.

IDENTIFICATION

Proper identification on your dog is important for his safety, as well as for your own peace of mind. If your Golden Retriever were ever lost or stolen, good ID could be the key to getting him back. The three most common types of ID are collar tags, tattoos, and microchip implants. There are pluses and minuses to each of these identification methods, so it's a good idea to equip your dog with more than one type of ID.

COLLAR TAGS: A plastic or metal ID tag fastened to your Golden Retriever's collar, with your contact information engraved on it, is a good first line of defense. Anyone finding your dog can easily read the tag and contact you directly. For security reasons you may choose not to list your name, your dog's name, or your home address on the tag, but the tag should include at least your home and cell phone numbers and perhaps your e-mail address. It's wise to list

Your Golden pup should wear an ID tag that includes your phone number.

your city and state of residence on the tag as well, so the person who finds your lost Golden can figure out how far from home your dog has traveled.

When vacationing with your dog, have a tag made that includes the phone number where you're staying and the number of a contact person who could be called in your absence. If there's no time to get a separate tag engraved with your vacation contact numbers, write them in waterproof pen on a piece of cloth adhesive tape, and stick it on top of his regular tag.

The drawback of tags is that they can be lost or deliberately removed, leaving no ID on your dog at all.

TATTOOS: This means of identification usually consists of a string of numbers and/or letters applied in permanent ink on the dog's inner thigh. The procedure takes only a few minutes and the sensation ranges from tickly to slightly painful, depending on the dog's sensitivity and the skill of the tattoo artist. The plus side of tattoo identification is its permanence: you can use the tattoo to prove that a "found" dog is yours. The downside is that, over time, the tattoo may become difficult to read, because the ink may fade or the characters may stretch as the dog grows.

For a fee, tattoo registries will keep a record of your dog's tattoo number and your contact information. Many people finding a dog would not know to look for a tattoo, however, and even if they did find it, they couldn't contact you directly to reunite you with your dog.

MICROCHIPS: This newer form of permanent identification is becoming increasingly popular. A small computer chip, the size of a grain of wild rice, is implanted under the skin between the dog's shoulder blades, through a special large-bore needle. Each microchip is coded

Dogs have worn collars for thousands of years, for adornment and identification as well as for control.

When vacationing with your dog, pack a clear photograph of him. If he gets lost, you'll have a picture available to make a lost dog poster.

The owners of some show and breeding dogs have DNA profiles created of their animals as a means of identification. However, this practice is rare among pet owners.

with a unique number, which is registered to the dog's owner through one of several microchip registries. If someone finds your lost Golden Retriever, the staff at nearly any veterinary clinic or shelter in North America should be able to scan the dog's back with a special microchip reader. The staff can then contact the microchip registry, so you can be contacted and reunited with your beloved pal.

SPAYING AND NEUTERING

Should you spay or neuter your Golden Retriever? For several decades, neutering pets by removing their reproductive organs has been considered the politically correct thing to do. According to the Humane Society of the United States, every year more than 3

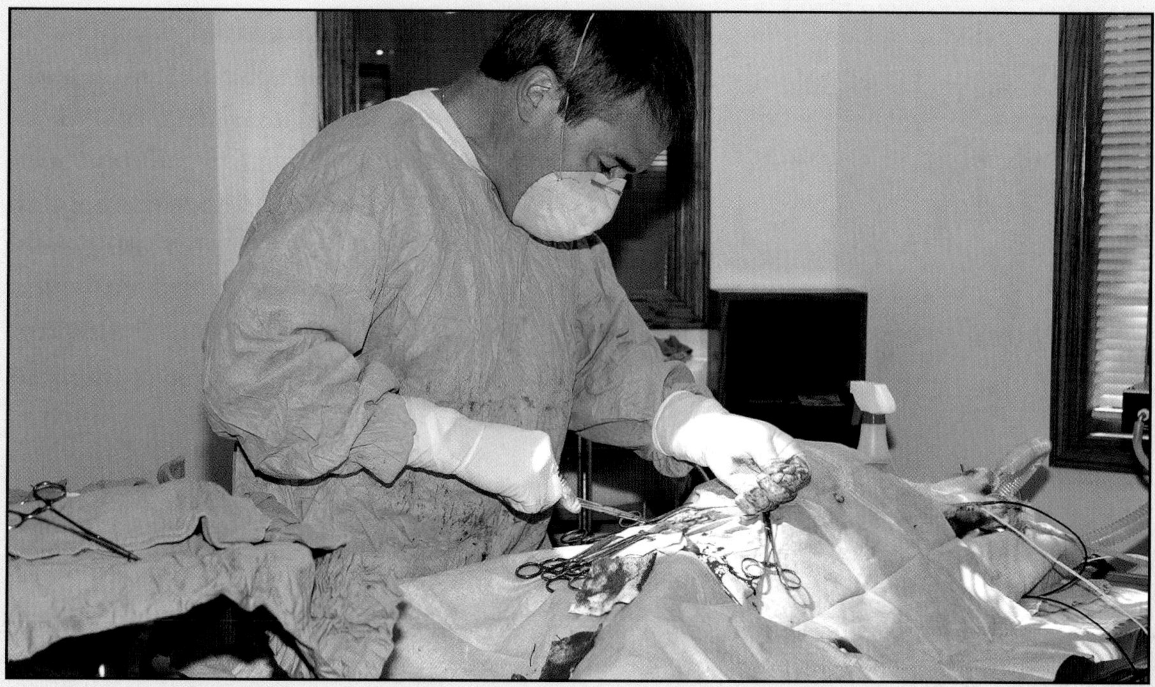

For most Golden Retriever owners, spaying or neutering is a wise decision. These procedures not only eliminate the possibility of unwanted puppies, they also provide health benefits for your dog.

Licensing an intact dog almost always costs more than licensing a spayed or neutered dog.

million unwanted dogs are euthanized in animal shelters. The practice of spaying females or neutering males is intended to address this problem by preventing the birth of unwanted pups.

There are other good reasons to consider spaying or neutering your pet. Removing your Golden Retriever's reproductive organs will eliminate some undesirable sexually driven behaviors. Intact male dogs are more likely to roam away from your property, especially if there's an intact female in the neighborhood. They also have a stronger tendency than their neutered counterparts to mark their territory with urine, to behave aggressively toward other dogs, or to "hump" the legs of visitors. Spaying a female Golden eliminates her estrous cycle (commonly known as being "in heat" or "in season"); in intact females, this can be accompanied by a messy discharge of blood. Spaying before the first heat cycle also eliminates the risk of ovarian or uterine cancer, and lowers a female dog's risk of developing mammary tumors and other diseases associated with the reproductive system.

However, in recent years, counterarguments have surfaced against across-the-board neutering. People who take this position advocate that pets should be neutered only after taking into account the individual animal's health and situation. They note that responsible owners can fairly easily confine their dogs to prevent unwanted litters, and that although some puppies are put to sleep, most animals euthanatized at shelters are adult dogs relinquished by their owners, not baby pups that couldn't find a home. In addition, some of the long-assumed health benefits of neutering have been called into question or shown to be false. For example, it was once believed that neutering would prevent prostate cancer in male dogs, but recent studies indicate that castrated males may actually have at as great or greater mortality risk as intact males for a particular form of prostate cancer. Nonetheless, neutered male dogs are much less likely to develop other common prostate problems as they age.

There are pros and cons to neutering, and dog owners need to educate themselves about both sides of this issue to make the best choice for their own Golden Retriever. But in light of recent studies on the effects of neutering, and with more studies in progress, neutering can no longer be viewed as the only responsible option for canine population control.

PET INSURANCE

A relatively recent development, pet insurance, will cover many of the bills if anything serious happens to your Golden Retriever, such as an accident or a major illness like cancer. If you have pet insurance, you won't have to make the difficult decision between treating your dog and putting him down because the treatment is too expensive. Several types of pet health insurance policies are available, and the right coverage could save you thousands of dollars in veterinary bills.

Veterinary health insurance for your Golden Retriever can be a huge financial help if he encounters serious medical problems, but there are numerous exclusions—procedures and tests the typical policy won't cover—so buyers should beware. For the most part, annual vet visits, vaccinations, and elective procedures such as teeth cleaning or spaying/neutering are not covered by these insurance policies. Preexisting medical conditions, and diseases common to the Golden Retriever breed, like dysplasia, are often excluded from these policies as well. Before purchasing a policy, read it carefully so you understand exactly what it covers and what's excluded.

LEGAL ISSUES

Just as you establish household rules so that you can live harmoniously with your dog in a human household, local and state governments establish laws so that your dog can live harmoniously in the community. Laws that

Not all pet insurance policies cover the same things. Before you sign on the dotted line, do research and make an informed decision.

Dog owners should always be considerate of their neighbors. Make sure that your dogs do not bark excessively when they are outside.

pertain strictly to pet ownership are designed to promote safety for both humans and animals, and to address conflicts that often arise between the two species.

Make sure you know about any laws in your community relating to dog ownership. Some communities limit the number of dogs you may keep on your property. This helps to minimize nuisance complaints and guards against animal hoarding situations.

General nuisance laws in your community may or may not have a provision addressing dog ownership in particular, but dogs that bark incessantly—whether indoors or out—are considered a nuisance. Don't leave your dog unattended outside to bark and disturb your neighbors. If your dog is an inveterate barker, you must train him to eliminate this behavior.

Your community may also have a leash law that requires your dog to

THE RIGHT SIDE OF THE LAW

Owning a large, powerful dog like a Golden Retriever means you may run up against legal issues that owners of smaller breeds never encounter. Some towns and cities have laws restricting certain dog breeds or the size and number of dogs a resident may legally own. As a breed, Golden Retrievers do not tend to be aggressive, but because they are large dogs they can sometimes be pretty boisterous. Even a friendly dog can get his owner in legal trouble if he playfully knocks a person down. Teach your Golden polite behavior around people, keep him leashed in stimulating situations, and know and abide by the dog laws in your locale and any place you vacation with your dog.

be on a leash any time he's off your property. This law is intended to encourage dog owners to keep their dogs under their control at all times. Dogs that are not under control can cause property damage, injuries, and even deaths. Under general liability laws, you are responsible for the actions of your Golden Retriever, whether those actions occur on or off your premises. Any problems with aggression, in particular, should be addressed with the help of a professional trainer.

Thanks to strict state requirements requiring rabies vaccinations for all dogs, rabies transmission from dogs to humans in the United States is now almost nonexistent. Unfortunately, this lethal virus still permeates the wild animal population, so it's crucial to have your dog vaccinated against rabies. Make sure you know what the requirements are in your state. Most states require an initial vaccination plus a three-year booster, while others require an annual rabies booster.

FAST FACT

According to the Centers for Disease Control in Atlanta, dogs bite about 4.7 million people in the United States every year. Of those bite victims, 800,000 require some form of medical attention.

CHAPTER FOUR

The Best Possible Beginning

While all Golden Retrievers share certain traits, no two individual Goldens are exactly alike. Some of them will be the kind of dog you're looking for, while others will have traits that don't appeal to you. Here are some tips to help you find a Golden Retriever that will be a good match for you.

FACTORS TO CONSIDER

GENDER: One important decision you need to make is whether you want a male or female Golden

When choosing a Golden Retriever, consider your family, lifestyle, and the size of your home. Doing research and making an informed choice will be best for everyone.

Retriever. Some people believe that male dogs make better hunters or that females are more affectionate, but these traits are not linked to gender. Both male and female Golden Retrievers can be equally affectionate and equally good workers.

Male Goldens are typically taller, more muscular, and stronger than females, and the male head is usually larger and broader. Some people are attracted to that larger size and stronger, more masculine appearance, so they choose a male. On the other hand, some people prefer the slightly smaller size and more feminine look of the female Golden.

Most adult Golden Retrievers make friends easily with other dogs, though some prefer the company of dogs of the opposite sex. If you already have a Golden and are getting ready to add another to your household, consider the way your current dog relates to other dogs. If your Golden doesn't get along well with dogs of the same gender, save yourself some frustration by choosing a new dog of the opposite sex. If your Golden gets along well with both sexes, he will probably readily accept a new housemate dog of either gender.

Your Goals: When you're considering acquiring a Golden Retriever, choosing one will be easier if you have some idea about what you'd like your dog to accomplish. Are you interested in participating in competitive sports, like Obedience, Agility, Tracking, or Field Trials? Would you like to exhibit your dog in Conformation shows? Would you like to get involved in pet-assisted t herapy by bringing your Golden to hospitals and nursing homes? To find a good candidate for any of these pursuits, seek out breeders whose dogs have excelled in the sports or activities that interest you most.

Good training and the right kind of stimulation can strengthen and enhance a dog's inherited potential, but for him to excel in a particular activity that potential must be present in the first place. You're more likely to find that potential in a pup whose parents and other relatives already demonstrate that ability. If you have a specific sport or activity in mind for a Golden Retriever you're considering, but are fairly new to that activity yourself, have someone with experience evaluate the pup or dog before you make a final decision.

HOW TO FIND A RESPONSIBLE BREEDER

The Golden Retriever Club of America (GRCA) has a code of ethics that offers guidelines for the care and breeding of Golden Retrievers. GRCA members who sign on to the code agree to maintain the highest standards of health, cleanliness, and care for their Golden Retrievers. This includes physical care, such as proper diet, exercise, and veterinary treatment, as well as psychological care, including training and socialization.

The breeder's code requires all dogs considered for breeding to first be x-rayed for hip and elbow abnormalities and certified that they don't have hereditary eye or heart abnormalities. Breeders provide their puppy buyers with complete health records for each pup, a four-generation pedigree, and the proper paperwork to register the dog. A puppy or dog from a breeder who adheres to the GRCA breeder's code should be clean, healthy, and confident. You'll have a better chance of finding a responsible and reputable Golden Retriever breeder if you choose from among those who are members in good standing of GRCA and have signed on to the breeder's code.

ADOPTING FROM A SHELTER OR RESCUE ORGANIZATION

Another option is adopting a dog from a shelter or rescue organization. Many lovely Golden Retrievers, through no fault of their

There are many adult Goldens that need "forever homes." Check the Internet for Golden rescue organizations near you.

Golden Retriever Rescue Organizations

Breeders and others who love Golden Retrievers volunteer their time, talents, and resources to help Goldens who find themselves homeless. Nonprofit breed rescue groups exist for most breeds. Some are small, independent, local rescues, while others are larger and more organized, with national and regional groups connected closely through a network of volunteers. There is a strong rescue network for Golden Retrievers.

Rescuing Golden Retrievers can be expensive, with the cost of veterinary care, food, transportation, equipment, phone, mailing expenses, and hundreds of other miscellaneous needs. Funds are quickly used up for the benefit of the dogs, and more money is always needed.

Animal-loving philanthropists will sometimes donate a large sum to a rescue organization, but most of the money for operating a breed rescue is raised by the groups themselves, by holding bake sales, garage sales, auctions, dog-walkathons, and whatever other fund-raisers they can think of to bring in needed donations.

Rescue groups always need more volunteers, and there are jobs for anyone willing to help out. Rescue organizations need volunteers to foster adoptable dogs, groom and exercise dogs, organize fund-raisers, check out the homes of prospective adopters and make follow-up visits after adoptions, help with paperwork and office chores, or even make a couple dozen cupcakes for a bake sale. If you can lend a hand to your local or regional Golden Retriever rescue group, it will be greatly appreciated, and it will help homeless Golden Retrievers.

own, are relinquished to shelters and rescue organizations. Dogs are given up for adoption for many reasons, and often they have nothing to do with any flaws in the dog himself. Most dogs are surrendered to shelters because of changes in the owner's situation. For example, the owner gets a job in a new town and cannot take the dog with her, a child in the family develops an allergy to the dog, or the owner dies and no one in the family wants her dog.

Some dogs end up in shelters and rescue organizations because the previous owner couldn't manage their behavior or temperament. Most of them are not rejects, however, just unfortunate victims of circumstance. You can find wonderful Golden Retrievers in shelters and rescues, and one might be the perfect companion for you.

When you adopt a dog from a shelter or rescue organization, there may not be much information available about his past. Ask the person handling the adoption to tell you as much as possible about the dog's behavior while he was in the organization's care. If you're not very experienced with Goldens, when you go to meet the dog you are thinking of adopting, take someone with you who is. If you don't have an experienced friend, consider hiring a dog trainer to evaluate the prospective adoptee for you. Make sure the trainer understands the qualities that are important to you, so she helps you pick the right dog.

Even though you've learned all you could about the dog and heeded the advice of experts, you could still be in for a few surprises after you've had your new dog for several months. Newly adopted dogs are often on their best behavior for about three months after the adoption. During that three-month period, the dog will settle in and get comfortable in his new home. Once he feels at home with you, he may start relaxing and behaving differently. Sometimes those "new" behaviors, which surface months after the adoption, are really old habits that got the dog into trouble with his last owner. As those behaviors appear, be prepared to manage the situation and the dog's environment while you teach him more acceptable behavior.

If you're determined to adopt a Golden Retriever puppy, you may have to wait a while to get one from a shelter or rescue organization; most of the dogs there will probably be adolescents or adults. There are some benefits to adopting more mature dogs, though. When you adopt an older dog, he may already be housetrained and know some obedience cues and other good skills, and you'll have a better idea of his temperament.

WHAT TO LOOK FOR IN A PUPPY AND ITS PARENTS

Before you go looking at litters of pups, think about the temperament and personality you'd like in your dog. Puppies are so cute that it's easy to fall in love with them, but not every pup will be right for you. Don't fall for the first pair of sweet brown eyes that cast their spell on you. Instead, handle and observe the pups for a while, then decide if one of them is the right animal companion.

By seven weeks old, a pup's natural personality and attitudes are fairly easy to recognize if you know what to look for. You can learn a lot about a puppy's temperament by observing him with his siblings. Watch how the puppies play with each other, and note which ones act bossy and which ones get bossed around. Place a large object, like an open cardboard box, in the puppy play area and watch what they do with it. Some pups will explore it, others may ignore it, and some may wait and watch what the others do and then mimic their actions. This experiment will give you an idea of how each pup approaches unfamiliar situations.

Observe the pups at play: how curious and how bold are they? Golden Retriever pups tend to retain the same personality and temperament traits as they mature, so imagine those traits in a grown dog and that will help you decide which pup would fit best your needs.

If the parents of the pups or any adult relatives are available, take a look at them, too. Puppies grow up resembling their relatives, so traits of body and temperament you see in the adults, you may also see in your pup when he

You can tell a lot about your puppy by the appearance and demeanor of his parents.

FAST FACT

If you have a purebred Golden Retriever but you don't have his registration papers, and would like to compete in Agility, Obedience, or other AKC events, apply for an Indefinite Listing Privilege (ILP). The American Kennel Club will issue your dog a number that will allow you to enter him in competition. Without papers, however, your dog will not be permitted to compete in Conformation events.

matures. If you have aspirations for competition events, seek a litter with parents that are accomplished in the events that interest you. Parent dogs with talent and drive are likely to produce offspring with potential for the same characteristics.

Dogs destined to be trained for Agility, Obedience, Conformation, and other competitive sports tend to do best if they are curious, bold, and very persistent. Not everyone wants or needs a dog like that, though. People who want Golden Retrievers mainly as companions usually prefer less intense dogs than people who train their dogs for competition in performance events.

CHOOSING A VETERINARIAN

Next to you, the veterinarian is your dog's most important ally in maintaining good health over his lifetime. If you don't already have a veterinarian for your pup, you need to find one and schedule a wellness exam. Don't wait until your dog really needs a veterinarian; instead, arrange for him to

Choose a veterinarian based on a number of factors: his location, his reputation, his skill, and of course, his rapport with your dog.

meet the veterinarian during a period of normal health. Being closely examined by a stranger can be scary, so meeting the veterinarian under pleasant conditions will help your Golden accept being handled by the doctor during future visits.

The American Kennel Club registers about 40,000 Goldens each year.

To find a good veterinarian for your Golden Retriever, start by asking your dog-owning friends and acquaintances, especially those with large dogs, which veterinarians they use. If several friends like and recommend the same veterinarian, that's a good sign.

Another sign to look for is the one on the veterinarian's reception counter that says AAHA. That stands for American Animal Hospital Association, an educational organization that helps those in veterinary practice to uphold the highest standards of animal care and accredits veterinary clinics that meet those standards.

Time is usually of the essence when a dog gets sick or injured, and if the veterinary clinic is far away, the trip to the clinic can use up precious time better spent with the doctor. So if you have a choice between a veterinarian who is within a fifteen-minute drive and one who is an hour away—all else being equal—it makes more sense to opt for the closer one.

Take into consideration whether your veterinary clinic is open twenty-four hours a day. If not, you'll need to make arrangements in case a medical emergency occurs during off-hours. Find out what your veterinarian's policies are for handling off-hours emergencies. Some veterinarians will rush from home at any hour and open the clinic for a patient with a true emergency, but that kind of service is rare and vanishing fast.

In some places, local veterinarians form an alliance to handle off-hours emergencies, each taking a turn on call overnight and on weekends and holidays. Many urban and suburban areas have emergency veterinary clinics that stay open 24/7, or clinics that are only open during off-hours.

Once you have lined up one or more veterinarians who sound good, plan a visit to the animal hospital for an interview and a hospital tour. Make an appointment for this and pay for the vet's time. Veterinarians are usually very busy, and any time they spend answering your questions is time they would otherwise spend with their animal patients.

CHAPTER FIVE

Caring for Your Puppy (Birth to Six Months)

To prepare for your new puppy, you'll need to get your home and your family ready for the new arrival. Establish the rules before you bring the pup home, and make sure all household members—including children—understand the rules and the reasons behind them. People tend

Both you and your new puppy have lots to learn in your first months together.

to follow rules better if they help formulate them, so ask family members for their input while you're planning for your puppy's imminent arrival.

Puppies explore their surroundings by playing with and chewing whatever draws their attention. This curiosity can be destructive, or even dangerous, if your home has not been puppy-proofed. This must be done before your new puppy comes into your home for the first time.

A pup's view of the world is different from yours; he sees everything from closer to the floor. Things look different from that perspective, so get down to puppy eye level and take a look around. Anything that sticks out or hangs down will immediately attract his attention, so remove those items or block your pup's access to them. Don't just make it challenging to reach those things, because Golden Retrievers enjoy meeting such challenges. Make it impossible.

PAPERS THE BREEDER WILL PROVIDE

When you buy a purebred Golden Retriever that can be registered, the breeder should give you all the paperwork necessary for registration when she sends the dog home with you. If you don't get all the paperwork when you pick up your Golden Retriever pup, it may be more difficult to get it later.

Here's the paperwork the breeder should give you when you get your puppy:

- The application form she got when she registered the litter, so you can register your pup yourself.
- A four-generation pedigree.
- The dog's vaccination and health certification records, such as Orthopedic Foundation of America (OFA) records of parents' orthopedic clearance and eye health of your puppy.
- Microchip and/or tattoo identification numbers, if applicable.

If the dog is an adult, the breeder should sign his registration over to you as his new owner.

WHAT TO EXPECT WHEN YOUR PUP FIRST COMES HOME

The first night home with a new Golden Retriever pup, often no one gets a full night's sleep. The puppy is used to sleeping with his littermates, so the first night without them he'll miss them and may whine or howl a sad lament for a while after you put him to bed.

To ease that loneliness, let him sleep in a crate or a pen in your bedroom. The pup will be comforted by

A blanket or towel that contains the scent of your new puppy's mother or littermates may help comfort your pup and enable him to sleep.

being able to see, hear, and smell your presence and won't feel so lonely in the unfamiliar new surroundings. It also helps to play soft music in the background when you put your Golden pup to bed. The music will soothe him so he'll be able to fall asleep eventually.

Here's another suggestion: play with your new pup for an hour or so before bedtime. That way, he'll be tired and will more likely fall asleep of his own accord.

PUPPY HEALTH

Hopefully, your puppy will be healthy when you get him, because once he enters your care, it will be up to you to keep him that way. Keeping a dog healthy takes work, but it's easier and less costly than treating a serious disease or injury. Make sure your pup gets everything he needs for good health, including clean water, nourishing food, daily exercise, timely immunizations, and regular veterinary exams.

Although some veterinary clinics do accept walk-in clients, most will require an appointment to see the doctor. When you get to the veterinary clinic, leave your dog in the car, if possible, while you check in at the front desk. There will be paperwork to fill out for the new patient's file, and that will be easier without an excited or worried pup on your hands.

Bring along the health records the breeder gave you as well as any medical information you have on your puppy's parents. The vet will be asking questions about your pup's medical history, and that information may be important.

When you check in, ask if the vet's appointments are running on schedule. Sometimes your veterinarian may get tied up with an emergency, so caring for that animal becomes the top priority. That emergency case will take time that wasn't scheduled and the day's appointments may start running late.

If you arrive early or find that an unscheduled emergency is causing a delay of more than fifteen minutes, keep your dog outside. He will probably stay calmer and be more comfortable if you sit in the car with him or take him for a walk instead of the two of you hanging around the waiting room. He'll also be less likely to contract illnesses from animals with contagious diseases in the waiting room. Be back in the clinic at least five minutes before your pup's turn with the veterinarian. Any time you leave the waiting area, tell the staff where you'll be, in case the doctor is ready sooner than expected.

WHAT TO EXPECT AT A VETERINARY EXAM

When the veterinarian examines your pup, she'll run her hands all over him. She'll palpate his abdomen, checking for hernias, muscle tone, and any lumps or irregularities. She'll feel his legs, hips, and elbows, and check for signs of dysplasia (a hereditary

At your first veterinary exam, your vet will look your puppy over carefully and evaluate his overall health.

malformation of the hip socket and/or the top of the thigh bone), as well as tenderness, or stiffness. She will check the pup's skin for lumps, bumps, flea dirt, or anything else that doesn't belong there. She will listen to his heart for murmurs and check the sound of his lungs. She will examine his ears and eyes and check his hearing and vision. She will look in his mouth and throat, and examine his teeth.

While the veterinarian examines your pup's body, she will also be observing his personality and degree of socialization. If she thinks your pup needs more socialization or practice with body handling, she may suggest ways to do that or refer you to a trainer or behavior specialist who can teach you what to do and help you do it.

If your puppy has not been wormed or if he shows any signs of parasites, such as frequent unformed feces or a habit of rubbing his butt on the floor, take a fresh fecal sample to the veterinarian so it can be checked under the microscope. Only a small amount of feces is needed for that; a sample the size of a thimble is plenty.

VACCINATIONS

After your Golden Retriever puppy gets a clean bill of health, he can receive any vaccinations that he needs at this stage of his development. Vaccinations for a number of diseases are recommended for all dogs because of the high risk of transmission and the serious health consequences they represent. These include distemper, parvovirus, rabies, parainfluenza, canine adenovirus, and leptospirosis. Additional vaccines are available to protect against diseases that are not considered universal risks, such as bordetella and Lyme disease.

Most of these diseases are viral and there is no cure for them, which means treatment is limited to addressing the symptoms with medications to alleviate vomiting and diarrhea, and providing supportive care in the form of intravenous fluids. Some of these diseases are very serious or even deadly for puppies, so it's crucial to have your puppy vaccinated according to the schedule recommended by the American Animal Hospital Association.

Among the diseases for which your Golden Retriever should be vaccinated are the following:

DISTEMPER: Distemper affects the nervous system and is fatal to 75 percent of infected puppies. Symptoms include eye and nasal discharge, severe listlessness, fever, vomiting and diarrhea.

PARVOVIRUS: Parvovirus is a highly contagious, gastrointestinal virus that causes high fevers, vomiting, and bloody diarrhea, and can also be fatal for puppies.

RABIES: By far, the most frightening and deadly of all dog diseases is rabies. This virus attacks the nervous system and causes symptoms ranging from throat paralysis and the inability to swallow (which causes the drooling commonly described as "frothing at the mouth") to delirium and hyperaggressiveness. Due to the seriousness of this disease, and its risk of transmission to humans, state laws require the vaccination of all dogs against rabies. Be sure to check with your vet about your state's requirements concerning this vaccination.

PARAINFLUENZA: Parainfluenza, a respiratory virus that is generally not serious in and of itself, can nonetheless reduce your puppy's immunity to secondary infections like pneumonia. Symptoms include coughing and nasal discharge.

CANINE ADENOVIRUS-2: Canine adenovirus-2 is an upper respiratory infection that causes a hacking cough. Although this virus is considered mild, the vaccine for this disease provides protection against a much more serious virus called canine adenovirus-1, also known as "infectious canine hepatitis." Canine adenovirus-1 causes the more serious consequences of jaundice and liver damage.

LEPTOSPIROSIS: Leptospirosis is a bacterial disease that can damage the liver and kidneys. Symptoms range from fever and jaundice to the excessive consumption of water. Because it's caused by bacteria, leptospirosis can be treated with antibiotics.

BORDETELLA: Also known as "kennel cough," bordetella is a common, highly contagious bacterial infection of the respiratory system that causes chronic coughing. This disease is not considered serious, but vaccination is recommended for dogs that come in contact with other dogs in a group setting, such as a kennel or a dog show. This optional vaccine is administered through an intranasal spray.

LYME DISEASE: Lyme disease can cause fever, loss of appetite, arthritis, listlessness, and joint swelling. This vaccine is only recommended for dogs that live in areas where deer ticks are prevalent.

Recent scientific studies have radically changed the thinking about canine immunizations. Veterinarians used to recommend immunizing all dogs once a year against every disease for which a vaccination existed. That protocol is being overhauled as this book goes to press, as major veterinary schools are calling for a new policy of fewer vaccinations, less frequent boosters, and tailoring an immunization protocol to the individual needs of each animal.

At this point, some veterinarians are still following the old vaccination protocol, while others have switched over to the new one. The best approach for a dog owner is to keep up with the news in this area. Until a consensus is reached on the best vaccination protocol, follow the guidance of the veterinarian who knows your dog best.

PUPPY NUTRITION

A Golden Retriever puppy needs a balanced diet. His food should be easy to digest, rich in high-quality proteins and fats, and contain all the vitamins and minerals needed to nourish his rapidly growing body. In the puppy's first few weeks, his mother's milk meets all these requirements. The mother dog's milk

During the first weeks after their birth, Golden Retriever puppies subsist solely on their mother's milk.

contains colostrum, which transfers to the puppies the mother's immunity to diseases for which she has been vaccinated. This maternal immunity lasts until the pups are between two and four months old, protecting the litter from dangerous viruses until they are old enough to receive vaccinations of their own.

When Golden Retriever puppies are about five or six weeks old, their mother will have trouble keeping up with their appetites. At this time the breeder will start feeding them soft solid foods, like baby cereal or ground meat thinned to a gruel with water or goat milk. When puppies first start lapping up this food, they usually end up wearing as much of it as they swallow. By the time you pick up your puppy, he will be fully weaned to solid food.

A Golden Retriever puppy needs plenty of protein and fat to support healthy growth and provide energy. Your pup can get the nutrients he needs from either a premium commercial dry food or from a diet of fresh meats, bones, and organs. Dry kibble is convenient and economical, and has the added benefit of helping to keep your Golden Retriever's teeth clean. When he crunches the kibble, it will scrape plaque and tartar off his teeth.

Choose a kibble formula for large-breed puppies, and make sure that it's made from high-quality ingredients. Avoid vegetable-based kibbles—dogs are carnivores and do better with a meat-based diet. (At least two of the first five ingredients listed must be meat in order for the food to qualify as meat-based.) Vegetable-based formulas, which are made mostly of rice, wheat, and corn, are less expensive per bag than meat-based foods. However, they will be more expensive in the long run, as you will have to feed your Golden Retriever more of the lesser-quality food per meal in order to meet his nutritional requirements. Vegetable diets are also very high in carbohydrates, which are difficult for dogs to digest.

Canned foods can be combined with the puppy's kibble, especially if he's having trouble chewing. These foods are made with one or two types of muscle meats or poultry, as well as animal by-products, grains, vitamins, and minerals. However, canned foods are more expensive than dry food.

More and more dog owners are starting to include fresh meat, bones, and vegetables in their dogs' diets. If you're interested in feeding your dog fresh foods, be sure to read up on proper nutrition, so you'll be giving your Golden Retriever puppy a well-balanced diet. A number of books feature healthy homemade diets for dogs, and several good Internet chat groups allow dog owners to exchange information and ideas about feeding Golden Retrievers fresh raw or home-cooked foods.

Another alternative is frozen dog foods, which are convenient for dog owners who don't have the time or the inclination to make balanced, home-prepared meals for their dogs. Frozen blends of fresh ground foods, formulated to supply most or all of the nutritional components a healthy dog needs, are sold at many pet food stores. Like canned foods, however, frozen dog foods are often expensive.

There is no one "best" diet for Golden Retriever puppies. People have strong preferences when it comes to dog food, but dogs can do well on a number of different diets. Between you and your veterinarian, you should determine the diet that your dog thrives on, and that's what you should feed him.

FEEDING SCHEDULE

Golden Retriever puppies need a lot of nutrients to keep up with their rapid rate of growth. That, plus all the energy these pups expend playing and exploring, makes it important for them to refuel frequently. It's best to feed your pup his meals at about the same times each day, spaced apart fairly evenly. The younger your pup, the more times a day he'll need to eat.

Until your puppy is about ten weeks old, he'll need at least four meals a day. From ten weeks to about four months, your puppy will eat three times a day, plus maybe a light snack at bedtime. After your puppy is four to five months old, he'll need two meals a day.

COGNITIVE DEVELOPMENT AND SOCIALIZATION

As the days and weeks go by, your Golden pup's brain will be growing and maturing, just as his body is. Your pup will begin to understand how his world works and how to make it work better. His attention span will grow longer, he'll figure things out more quickly, and he'll be able to learn new skills and do more with what he knows.

Socialization is one of the most important things you need to do to prepare your Golden pup for a happy and confident adulthood. The more people, animals, and new situations a puppy encounters, the more confident and accepting he will be as an adult. The reason for socialization training is to help the pup discover that the world is a friendly place, for the most part, and that the people, animals, and situations he will

Golden Retrievers typically love people. Socializing your dog as much as possible will help him develop proper behavior skills.

encounter are interesting but generally harmless.

Be careful not to overstimulate your pup. Figure out how much he can handle, and avoid pushing him past that point. Overwhelming him with too much at once may backfire badly and create fear instead of dispelling it.

Introduce your puppy to between three and five new friendly people a week. The people should represent as many variations of the human form as possible. Let your pup meet tall, short, old, and young people. Introduce him to men with facial hair; women with big hats; kids on skates, scooters, and boards; runners and hikers; bicyclists and people with motorcycles; folks of all sizes, shapes, and colors. Make sure the people he meets are friendly and gentle, and don't let them do anything that frightens him.

Dogs need friends, too! Dog parks and puppy kindergarten are good places to introduce your Golden Retriever to other dogs and people in the area.

If you want your Golden to be protective of your family and property, it's just as important to socialize him to lots of friendly strangers. He will learn that when you want him to be friends with someone, you will deliberately introduce him. He will view those people as friends because you are there telling him they are and making sure they stay friendly. When he matures, he will recognize the difference between people you tell him are friends and people who sneak and trespass and behave very differently than "friends" do. Socializing your Golden will make him a better, more discerning protector than if he distrusted all people outside the family.

Socialization includes introducing your pup to friendly dogs, cats, and other pets, and large animals like horses, cows, and llamas. For the animal socialization, choose carefully, because if a "friendly" animal intimidates or hurts the pup, he may lose faith in your ability to know the difference between safe and unsafe.

A puppy kindergarten class is a great place for your Golden pup to meet and play with other dogs his age. You and the class instructor will both be there to make sure the play goes well and no pups bully others. Playtime and lesson time alternate in a good puppy kindergarten class, so your pup learns to come and pay attention to you, even when several puppy pals are nearby.

For animals other than dogs, it is often safest to let the pup see, hear, and smell them but not allow physical contact, particularly if the animals are not yours and you don't know if they're gentle with pups. Go near enough to them so that your pup can satisfy his curiosity, but keep far enough away so everyone remains safe.

Some people avoid taking their pups out to socialize and meet the world until they have all their immunizations. Unfortunately, by that time the main window of opportunity for socializing a pup has usually passed, and the pup may have developed a fear of the unfamiliar. It's a longer and more complicated process to socialize a puppy that has been isolated most of his first six months.

GROOMING

Golden Retrievers shed huge amounts of hair during their twice-yearly coat changes, and those each

A Golden's thick fur needs regular brushing to avoid knots and mats.

generally last a month or more. To keep your Golden looking tidy, and to reduce the amount of loose fur clinging to your clothing and carpets, you'll need to brush your Golden every day while he's shedding, and then twice a week year round.

Your puppy's coat is soft and wooly compared to the coat he will have as an adult. His adult coat will keep him warm and dry in nasty weather, but his puppy coat won't. Until your Golden's soft puppy fur is replaced with the weather-resistant double coat of an adult, you'll need to protect him from wet, chilly weather and dry him thoroughly if he goes out in the rain.

BRUSHING AND BATHING

Dogs don't sweat the way humans do; therefore, they don't need to bathe as

Your Golden Retriever will need a bath approximately every two months—or whenever he starts to smell!

frequently. However, it's important to keep your dog's skin and coat clean with routine brushing and bathing. Your Golden Retriever will feel better when he's clean, and he will also be more likely to attract positive attention and affection from others.

The natural oils in a Golden Retriever's coat make it lustrous, but they also give the coat a slight odor that intensifies with time, heat, and moisture. Natural coat oils also attract dirt and grime from the environment, which will eventually make the coat feel somewhat sticky. If you brush your Golden Retriever's coat thoroughly several times a week, he will look and smell acceptable. However, no matter how often you brush him, he will eventually need a soap-and-water bath.

Many dogs dislike baths, but it's possible to make bathing less distasteful for your dog if you go about it the right way. Here are some tips to help you accomplish that:

- Prepare the tub by placing a nonskid rubber mat on the bottom, so your dog will have good traction and not hurt himself by slipping and sliding.
- Keep the drain open and don't fill the tub. Dogs usually prefer this to standing in slippery, soapy water.
- Take a couple dozen small yummy treats into the bathing area with you, and dole them out to your Golden Retriever puppy every few minutes during his bath.
- Place some cotton balls in your dog's ears so water doesn't get into his ear canals.
- Wet down your dog's coat with wrist-temperature water (cooler than people usually like for bathing), using the shower wand or a plastic pitcher. Try not to get your Golden Retriever's head wet yet. Once a dog's head gets wet, he will want to shake the water off. Waiting until the end to wash his head and face will keep you drier during the bathing process.
- Put about a quarter-cup (60 ml) of shampoo in a gallon (4 liter) jug and fill the jug with lukewarm water. Use this diluted shampoo as the soap for your Golden Retriever; diluted shampoo will be much easier to work into his fur than full-strength shampoo. Also, you will use less shampoo this way and it will take less time and water to rinse it out of the coat.
- Apply the shampoo and lather it through the coat, starting at the neck and working toward the tail.

Keep your dog's head and face dry until the end of the bath, and any time water is splashed on his face, quickly wipe it off with a dry towel.

- Rinse your dog, starting with his neck and working back toward his tail. Rinse him until the water running down the drain is clear and has no more bubbles. Then rinse him one more time. If you leave any shampoo in his coat, it will attract dirt and become sticky and stinky, and your dog will need another bath much sooner than he would otherwise.
- Dry your Golden Retriever as thoroughly as possible with towels, then finish the job with a blow dryer set on low or cool. If you don't use a hair dryer, it will take hours for your Golden to dry all the way to his skin. In warm weather this is not generally a problem, but if you let him go outside in cool weather before his undercoat is completely dry, he can get a bad chill.

When bathing your Golden Retriever, you should use shampoo that is formulated for dogs.

NAIL CARE

Your Golden Retriever's nails need to be trimmed regularly or they will grow excessively long and sharp. Long toenails can deliver a nasty scratch, and they can start growing in a curve that will tend to get snagged on things and be torn off. This is very painful for the dog, so avoid that possibility by making it a habit to trim your dog's nails frequently.

Nail trimming should optimally be done every week, but a trim every two weeks can still keep a Golden Retriever's nails in good shape. If you let it go longer than that, though, the blood vessels and nerves in the living tissue (called the quick) inside the nail will grow out too close to the end of the nail. This will make it difficult to trim your dog's nails without nicking the quick and causing the dog pain.

You can trim your dog's nails with special scissors or clippers made for pet nails. If you don't feel confident using tools with blades on your dog's nails, you could file them down by hand instead, with a convex file specially designed for dogs' nails. If that's too slow for you, try shortening your Golden Retriever's nails with an electric rotary tool, similar to those used in nail salons.

To trim the nails, support the dog's paw and steady the toe you're working on. Trim off just the tip of the nail. Don't cut too much off, or you'll hurt the dog. If you cut too deep, you'll nick the blood vessels that feed the nail, causing bleeding and pain. Commercial blood coagulant powders are available at pet supply stores. These powders will quickly stop a nail from bleeding when it's cut too short. Buy some and keep it on hand, just in case.

DENTAL CARE

Clean teeth and healthy gums are important to your Golden Retriever's health. Food residue that remains on teeth after eating promotes the growth of bacteria and the formation of plaque. When a dog's teeth become caked with hardened plaque and the gums become infected, simple bad breath is the least of the concerns. Bacteria from gum infections can find their way into the bloodstream and travel to the heart. If that bacteria infects the dog's heart valves, serious illness or death may result.

Some dogs can keep their teeth fairly clean by chewing on kibble, bones, or chew toys, but often that's not clean enough for optimal health. Brushing your Golden Retriever's teeth regularly can help prevent plaque buildup. Use a toothpaste specially formulated for dogs, as human toothpastes contain chemicals that can be harmful to your Golden and he won't like the minty flavor anyway. You can either use a special dog toothbrush or a finger brush to clean his teeth. The finger brush slides over your finger like a glove and has bristles that enable you to scrub your dog's teeth. These work very well with large-breed dogs like Golden Retrievers.

Once plaque has hardened, you may not be able to remove it by brushing. When this happens, the dog should have his teeth cleaned by the veterinarian. Many dogs need a professional dental cleaning annually, and some need cleaning twice a year. Keep an eye on your dog's mouth. If you see a hard whitish, brownish, or yellowish buildup on your dog's teeth at the gum line, schedule a professional cleaning.

HOUSETRAINING

All dogs need to learn the manners required for living with humans. Teaching clean elimination habits is one of the first training challenges

The chemicals in some new carpeting may exude an ammonia smell, which can trigger a dog to urinate there.

THE POTTY BELL

One common cause of housetraining accidents is a pup's inability to let his people know when he needs to go outside. You can resolve this issue easily by teaching your Golden Retriever puppy to ring a bell when he needs to go outside to eliminate.

Hang a bell on a cord and tie it around the handle of the door closest to your pup's outdoor potty area. You won't have to teach your pup to ring it; just ring it yourself before opening the door each time you take him out to eliminate.

Your Golden pup will soon make the connection between the bell ringing and the door opening, and will wonder if the bell causes the door to open. Within about a week after you start ringing the bell, he will give it a try himself. When he does, praise him and open the door for him. Once he realizes that he can "make" you do that by ringing the bell, he'll use it whenever he needs to go out.

you'll face with your Golden Retriever pup, but you can make housetraining easier by establishing a consistent routine. Put your pup on a regular eating schedule and he'll have more predictable elimination times. Give him frequent opportunities to use the designated potty area; that will help prevent messy accidents in the house.

Teach your Golden Retriever a cue word or phrase for elimination. Pick something you won't be embarrassed to say when you're out in public. Popular cues are "Go potty," "Do business," or "Hurry up." Say the cue when your pup is in the area you want him to use. Wait patiently until he goes, then quietly and calmly praise him.

When your pup has potty accidents—and all pups do—don't scold

Children follow rules better when they're allowed to help make them up. Include your children in the rule-making process about what the pup is allowed to do and how the pup should be treated.

Golden Retrievers have incredibly expressive eyes. As you get to know your Golden, you'll discover that as he becomes housetrained, he'll give you a certain "look" when he needs to go outside to do his business.

or punish him. Scolding can make your pup avoid you when he has to eliminate, but he needs your help to get outside.

If you see your Golden pup start to eliminate indoors, call his name, clap your hands, or say something to get his attention. Then tell him, "Outside! Potty outside!" and quickly escort him to the approved area. At the potty place, calmly encourage him to eliminate, and then praise him when he does. Don't punish him for eliminating in an improper place.

If you don't catch your pup in time and you discover a potty accident after the fact, get a paper towel and take the pup back to the accident spot.

Don't scold or shame him, just calmly blot up the pee or pick up the poop in the paper towel, then gently escort your pup to the elimination area. Smear the pee or drop the poop there, then step back and calmly praise your pup, "Good potty outside," as you would if he had gone there to begin with. Your puppy will learn that there's a "good place" to do potty business, and with your help and patience he will learn to use that area.

ESTABLISHING HOUSEHOLD RULES

The best time to establish household rules is when you first get

If you don't want your Golden on the couch as an adult, this rule must be consistently enforced when he is a puppy.

your pup. Don't allow your puppy to do things you wouldn't find acceptable in an adult Golden Retriever. If you start with one set of rules now, and then try to change them when your pup gets older, that will confuse him. It's much harder to change an ingrained habit than to establish a good one right from the start, so think about how you'll want your Golden Retriever to behave as an adult, and help him learn those behaviors while he's young and impressionable.

If, for example, you allow your pup to sit on furniture, he'll want to lounge there as an adult. If you're sure that will be okay with you, go ahead and invite him onto the couch. However, if you don't want an adult Golden Retriever on your sofa or bed, set that rule while your pup is young and stick to it.

Consistency is one of the hallmarks of good training technique. Make sure you give your Golden Retriever pup consistent guidelines to follow, and enforce the rules you set up fairly.

CHAPTER SIX

Things to Know as Your Puppy Grows (Six Months to Two Years)

From six months to two years of age, a Golden Retriever develops from an awkward adolescent into a graceful, well-proportioned adult. During this period, the dog's bone growth slows, then stops, and the bones finish hardening.

HEALTH ISSUES

If you followed your veterinarian's vaccination protocol during your pup's

As your Golden grows, his face will change, taking on the characteristics of an adult dog.

first six months, your Golden Retriever should be finished with vaccinations for the year. Many veterinarians suggest annual boosters for all vaccinations, though studies currently in progress show that yearly boosters may be unnecessary, and they can be hard on some dogs' immune systems. The advice you follow about vaccination schedules should come from a veterinarian you trust.

When you visit your veterinarian, he will look for the emergence of health problems in your growing Golden Retriever. Every breed has some health conditions that occur more frequently than average in that breed. Some of these conditions are hereditary, while others are just related to the breed's size or shape. Your veterinarian will also check your Golden to make sure he's not infected with internal or external parasites.

Among the conditions that are more common in Golden Retrievers than in many other breeds are the following:

PANOSTEITIS: This condition appears in some Golden Retrievers or other large-breed dogs before they are two years old. Panosteitis, or "wandering lameness," is a growth condition of the leg bones that can cause lameness. It will often move from one leg to another, then suddenly disappear, and then days or weeks later return just as suddenly. Although this condition can be treated, most dogs with panosteitis make a full recovery, even without treatment.

PARASITES: Dogs should be checked for internal parasites at least once a year. If that hasn't been done since your dog was tiny, you should take in a fecal sample and have the veterinarian check for worms again. Young pups, elderly dogs, and unhealthy dogs all tend to build up large populations of various worms in the digestive tract. Worms seldom bother healthy, strong adults, but your Golden Retriever should be checked and given deworming medicine, if needed.

If you see evidence of fleas on your Golden Retriever—frequent scratching, chewing on the rump at the base of his tail, or dark red or blackish "dirt" in that same area (that dirt is flea feces)—give your pet a flea bath as soon as possible.

Fleas prefer dining on sick or weakened individuals, but they will happily bite healthy creatures, too.

If you see dark red or blackish "dirt" on the skin of your dog's rump, it may be flea feces. To find out, drop a few grains of it into a tablespoon of water. If the water turns red, that's your Golden's blood in that flea poop.

Most flea collars don't work very well on large dogs, but several brands of liquid antiflea treatment, which are applied to the back of the dog's neck or withers, are good on most dogs. Veterinarians generally stock and dispense various brands of flea treatments, and several of these products are also available, without prescription, from pet supply stores and catalogs.

Another external parasite, the tick, is known to transmit a number of potentially devastating diseases to both dogs and humans, including Lyme disease. Ticks are small, flat parasites that burrow their tiny heads into their host's skin to subsist on blood. They are particularly attracted to the blood-rich skin of a dog's ears and face. If you find a tick on your dog, it should be removed as quickly as possible by grasping the tick close to the head with tweezers and then pulling it off. The longer a tick remains embedded in your dog's skin, the greater the chance it will transmit a tick-borne disease to your dog!

Heartworm: Heartworm is a serious health problem for dogs in most areas of the United States, but it's worst in moist, warm climates with large populations of mosquitoes. As its name suggests, heartworm is a worm that lives in the heart.

Mosquitoes carry heartworm. When a dog is infected with heartworm, a microscopic, immature stage of the heartworms (called microfilaria) circulates through the dog's bloodstream. If a mosquito bites the infected dog, along with its blood meal it draws in some microfilaria as well. If that mosquito bites another dog, some microfilaria will be injected into that new victim, where they will continue their life cycle and, in about three months, migrate into the heart itself and develop into adult worms. Within six to eight months, these adults begin

Most canine internal parasites cannot be seen in the stool by the naked eye. They must be detected through microscopic examination.

THE DANGER OF HEARTWORMS

Heartworms are a concern for all dog owners. The graphic above illustrates the cycle of heartworm development. When a mosquito (1) bites a Golden Retriever, it can inject microfilaria into his bloodstream. The microfilaria travel through the bloodstream to the heart (2), where they grow into heartworms (3) and multiply, clogging the dog's heart. If left untreated, heartworms can kill.

to reproduce, adding more heartworms to the dog's growing load.

Each adult worm can reach a length of 12 inches (30.5 cm) or more. If a tangle of these worms clogs a dog's heart, it cannot pump efficiently, so the dog becomes weak and sick. A heavy load of heartworms, left untreated, will bring on the dog's death.

Administering prescription medications that kill the microfilaria before they develop into adult heartworms can prevent heartworm infection. The preventive must be used just before mosquitoes appear in spring until they go dormant for winter. In some parts of the country, mosquitoes stay active year round, so dogs must remain on preventive heartworm medication all year long. Your veterinarian can advise you on the best preventive regimen for your area.

Before dogs are given heartworm preventives, they must be tested to make sure they're not already infected. It can be fatal to administer preventive heartworm medication to a dog with adult heartworms. A different regimen is needed to clear up a heartworm infection. Because treating heartworm infection is dangerous, and sometimes fatal, it's much better to prevent infections from occurring.

NUTRITION

Your Golden Retriever is heading into adulthood at this stage. By one year of age, he has reached his adult height, but he's still building muscle mass, so he still needs nutrition for a growing dog. His food should be rich in highly digestible forms of protein and fat, as well as vitamins and minerals, for muscle-tissue growth, overall health, and high energy.

Pick a high-quality food that is made for large-breed dogs. Cheaper foods contain too much fat or vegetable protein, and this can lead to an unhealthy growth spurt. Another problem with feeding your Golden food that has lower-quality ingredients is that vitamin and mineral deficiencies can contribute to skeletal complications, such as hip or elbow dysplasia. An expensive price tag does not guarantee excellence, though, so always read the ingredient list. Ideally, meat should be among the first few ingredients listed in any dog food.

Your dog's stomach is now large enough for him to be fed all the nutrition he needs in two meals a day. If he likes a bedtime biscuit, he can certainly have that, too. As long as he's eating the right food, not

Feed your Golden Retriever a high-quality dog food to ensure his good health.

overindulging in treats, and getting plenty of exercise, you won't have to worry that he's gaining too much weight.

SOCIALIZATION

Socialization means exposing your puppy to all kinds of people, places, things, and animals, so he can learn that the world is an interesting and mostly safe place. Take your pup on outings to new places and to meet new people several times a week. Don't overdo it, however; keep outings shorter than two hours, and be ready to head home if you think your pup is getting overstimulated or tired. The more friendly people your Golden meets as a puppy, the more confident he will be as an adult and the more socially appropriate his behavior will be throughout his life.

If you have adopted a Golden in this age group who has not been well socialized, it's important to help him catch up on his social skills with people and with other dogs. The more mature a young dog becomes,

Properly socializing your Golden with other people and animals will allow you to take your best friend with you just about anywhere.

the more he thinks he already knows. If he doesn't get used to people and animals and other things he'll encounter in the "big world" outside your home, he may become fearful of them.

An adolescent or young adult Golden that hasn't met many people may be shy when he encounters new people. A shy or timid Golden may hide his uncertainty and fear behind a façade of loud, aggressive-sounding barking. A Golden not used to other dogs may put on that same kind of loud barking display. Unfortunately, all the adrenaline the dog works up barking so fiercely may actually increase his fear. Fear can cause a dog to try to defend himself by fleeing or biting, either of which can actually make the dog more vulnerable.

If your Golden reacts to someone or something fearfully, whether with a show of self-protective aggression, or by trying to escape, do not scold, do not whimper reassurance, and do not try to make him "face his fears." The best thing you can do is to calmly walk your dog farther from the "scary thing." Go with him far enough from the source of his fear that he no longer feels the need to flee or bark, and then just stand or sit there with him for a while and let him observe the "scary thing" from this safe distance. Speak calmly and describe what he is watching out loud, in a matter-of-fact tone of voice. "That's Ben. He's riding his bicycle. He's very tall. He's wearing a purple hat"—that sort of pattern. Your calm tone of voice, your relaxed posture, and the increased distance from the scary thing will all put your Golden at ease and allow him to realize that there is no reason to be afraid. Only reapproach scary things after your Golden seems relaxed. You cannot force a fear to go away, but you can help it fade more quickly by making it seem less scary through your own calm reactions.

PROPER EXERCISE

By six months of age your Golden Retriever will be more than half his adult size and will have the energy of two adult dogs. At this age he needs vigorous exercise every day—not just a walk around the block on a leash at your pace, but running free at dog speed, someplace where he can stretch his legs and gallop.

Make sure that the place where you let your Golden run for exercise is far from traffic and other hazards. A galloping Golden Retriever can travel very quickly. Don't turn your dog loose if he hasn't yet learned to always come when called. Until he

It's important to give your Golden plenty of "off-the-leash" time where he is allowed to run freely in a safe area. However, only set him loose when he's been trained to respond immediately to your commands.

responds more reliably, exercise him in a safely fenced area.

BASIC OBEDIENCE TRAINING

You should have started teaching your puppy good manners and obedience the day you brought him home. This training will continue for the rest of his life. Dogs learn the rules of life by paying attention to what works and what doesn't, so you're training your dog every time you interact with him.

If you haven't yet taken your Golden to obedience school, don't wait any longer to enroll in a class. By the time your Golden Retriever is six months old, he'll think he knows how life works. Get him into training soon and teach him that wonderful things come to good dogs that do as they're told.

To find a reputable trainer, ask for recommendations from your veterinarian and your friends who own dogs. Training classes can be a lot of fun if you like the instructor and her methods. When you get some leads on trainers near you, call them and make arrangements to observe one of their classes without your dog, so you'll see how they relate to both two-legged and four-legged students.

Some Golden Retriever owners like to train their dogs themselves. You can train a dog to do just about anything you'd like, but initially you should focus on some basic obedience commands: "sit," "down," "stay," and "come." These commands will provide a foundation for any other type of training you have in mind.

Sit: Sitting is such a natural position for dogs that your Golden may adopt this position on his own. If you reward him with praise or treats each time he does it, and eventually add the "sit" command, you can teach your dog to sit at your whim. If your dog can't figure it out quite this easily, you can help him into the sit position by holding a treat above his head, just behind his eye level. When he looks up to keep his eyes on the treat, his back end may naturally drop into a sit. If not, you can further assist your dog by scooping his back legs underneath him. Plenty of repetition and generous rewards when he gets it right will have your dog sitting like an Obedience competition champ.

Golden Retrievers are extremely smart dogs. They tend to pick up tricks very easily. With just a bit of practice, your dog will learn a variety of commands.

Down: You can teach your dog to lie down on command by starting from the sit position. Hold a treat on the floor in front of your dog and slowly drag it away from him. This will encourage your dog to stretch out his head and front feet as he tries to keep his nose close to the treat. If your dog stretches out even a little bit, reward him with the treat. Even if your dog has not yet reached a full down position, you should reward any movement he makes in the right direction, as many obedience skills are best taught in small increments.

If your dog stands up or gets out of position, put him back into a sit and start over. A lot of patience, combined with small enough "baby steps," will eventually result in the desired behavior. Then, you can begin using the "down" command so your dog can learn to associate this word with the correct position.

Stay: The "stay" command is very useful for controlling the movement of your dog, especially in situations where safety is a concern. This command involves two components—distance and duration—that must be taught in increments. You can work on both at the same time, provided you take this training slow and don't push your dog to progress faster than he is ready.

With your dog in a sitting position, tell him to "stay," take one step away from him, and then step toward him immediately. If your dog has maintained his sitting position, reward him. Repeat this a couple times. When your dog remains seated consistently when you take one step away, you can advance to two steps away, and so on. Gradually increase both

Once your Golden learns to sit, the "down" and "stay" commands should be easy for him to master.

the distance and the duration. If your Golden breaks his stay at any point, it's an indication that you're expecting too much too fast. Back up a few steps and progress more slowly.

The "stay" command will become a little more challenging for your dog when you are ready to practice out-of-sight stays. Your dog likes to know where you are at all times, and the minute you step out of the room, he'll attempt to follow you. Set your dog up for success by stepping out of the room for only a fraction of a second in the beginning. Return immediately to reward your dog. This way, your dog will learn that you fully intend to come back, and he'll be a little more patient in waiting for longer periods of time.

Come: The "come" command is the most important skill you can teach your dog. A dog that does not come when called is an accident waiting to happen. That's why you should practice "come" every chance you get. Keep some treats in your pocket and call your dog from different rooms in your house at different times of the day. Call your dog only once each time and reward him whenever he responds. If he doesn't come on the first call, he gets no reward.

You can practice "come" outdoors in a fenced area or on a long leash, but again, only call your dog once each time and only reward your dog when he responds immediately. Don't force your dog to come to you by pulling on his leash, or he will quickly learn that "come" is only mandatory when he's on a leash. Instead, coax your dog to you by calling him in a happy voice or running a few steps away from him to encourage him to chase you.

The whole purpose of practicing the "come" command constantly is to condition your dog to respond automatically, without thinking about it, so that he will eventually listen to you even in the face of distractions. The "come" should always be presented in an upbeat manner, because if you scold or punish your dog when he doesn't come immediately, he won't be in much of a hurry to come to you the next time!

TRAVELING WITH YOUR GOLDEN

Golden Retrievers like to be with their people, and can easily become seasoned travelers. Most Goldens enjoy car rides, and adapt well to longer trips. On a long road trip, make sure to schedule regular stops where your dog can stretch, sniff around, and go to the bathroom. Make sure your Golden is securely fastened, either with a dog seatbelt, in his crate, or behind a vehicle barrier.

When traveling, plan your overnight accommodations in advance. Not all hotels or motels will accept pets, particularly larger dogs like Golden Retrievers. Look for establishments that claim to be "pet friendly," and make sure to ask whether there will be extra fees to allow your dog to stay in the room.

Pack a travel bag for your Golden that includes food, bowls, toys, treats, any medication he needs, and a first-aid kit. You should also bring his bed or a blanket for him to sleep on, identification tags, and his leash. If you'll be vacationing with your Golden Retriever far from

Golden Retrievers love to ride in the car. For your dog's safety, however, always be sure he is properly restrained while the car is in motion.

TRAVEL SAFETY

Traveling with your dog is fun, as long as you keep your dog safe!

- Make sure your dog is up-to-date on vaccinations.
- Obtain any additional vaccinations your dog may need, depending on your travel destination. For example, if you'll be staying where Lyme disease is prevalent, you may want to get a shot.
- Bring a photo of your dog, together with any health documentation, such as a rabies vaccination certificate.
- Keep a collar and ID tag on your dog at all times, and keep him on a leash.
- Make sure your dog is microchipped prior to your trip.
- Don't forget to bring any medications your dog requires.
- A canine first aid kit is a must for campers.

home, have a special ID tag made that includes your local phone number or a cell phone number. This way you can be reached if your Golden wanders off and gets lost.

It's usually easier and more pleasant for dogs to travel by automobile than by airplane. Often, dogs traveling by plane must be carried in a crate in the cargo hold of a jet. However, Golden Retrievers that have flown a few times usually settle into their crates calmly and tolerate the flight well. When booking your flight, ask if the airline has any special program for transporting live animals, or if there are any factors that you need to consider when bringing him along on your trip.

LEAVING YOUR GOLDEN AT HOME

There are times you may have to travel without your Golden Retriever, such as on a business trip. When you must leave your Golden Retriever behind, there are several care alternatives to choose from. If you have friends or relatives who are willing to take good care of your dog, you might be able to leave him with them or have them come stay at your home. That would be a great solution.

However, many people don't have friends or relatives able or willing to take on that responsibility.

In that case, there are pet sitters for hire who will visit your dog two or more times a day, feeding, exercising, grooming, and even medicating the dog, if necessary. Some pet sitters will stay overnight at your home and care for your pets almost the way you would. They charge more for that kind of service, but for some dog owners—especially those with multiple pets—whatever the overnight sitter charges is worth the cost.

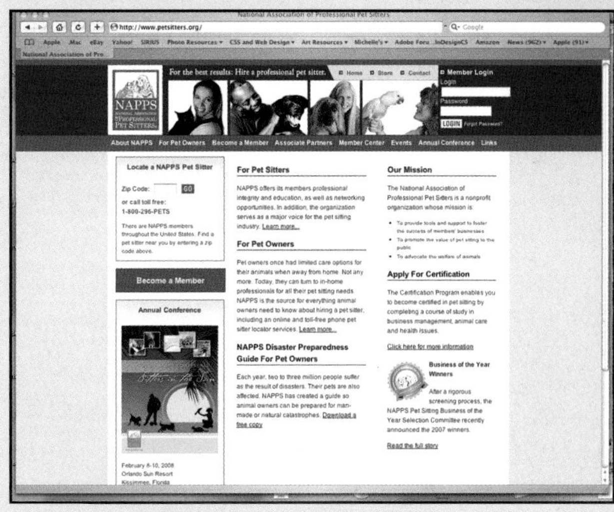

The Web site of the National Association of Professional Pet Sitters, www.petsitters.org, can be used to help you find the right person to watch your pet while you're away.

If you're traveling, or even if you're just away from home for long days all week and find that you don't have much time or energy to exercise your dog when you get home, consider doggy day care. At day care facilities, dogs are dropped off in the morning and picked up later the same day. Some day care centers have vans to pick up the dogs and take them home, saving the owners that trouble.

Keep in mind that dogs with aggressive attitudes toward either people or other dogs are not good candidates for doggy day care. It will be stressful for them to be around nonfamily humans and dogs all day, and they will escalate the stress level of everyone else, both human and canine. Dogs that get along well with others can have a lot of fun at day care, however. Dogs that like people but not other dogs may enjoy being walked, petted, and played with by the staff.

Boarding kennels are mainly for overnight stays, though many offer doggy day care as well. Most boarding kennels keep the dogs in runs or cages most of the time, walking them on-leash for a bit of exercise or turning them out into a fenced area to walk around and sniff on their own. A dog that dislikes other dogs may not fare well at a kennel, unless his run is blocked visually from a view of other dogs. A dog that isn't good with people may do fairly well at some kennels, but it depends on how skilled the staff is in dealing with that type of dog.

CHAPTER SEVEN

Caring for Your Adult Dog

Golden Retrievers become calmer and less boisterous as they mature, but as adults they still like to play and they still need plenty of exercise to stay fit. Once a Golden reaches full maturity, he may start gaining weight if he eats too much and doesn't get enough exercise.

Dogs like Goldens, which are bred to work, really need something constructive to do with their abundant physical energy; otherwise, they'll get bored and restless. They also require mental stimulation. Advanced training for competition events like Obedience, Agility, or

Golden Retrievers are "people" dogs, and they want nothing more than to be with their masters.

Rally makes a good substitute for a "real" job. (Advanced training will be discussed on pp. 81–88.)

HEALTH ISSUES

Your adult Golden Retriever should have a veterinary checkup at least once a year. During these visits the veterinarian will take your dog's temperature and listen to his heart and lungs. She will look into your dog's eyes and ears, examine his mouth, teeth, and gums, and feel his body all over for lumps, swellings, or anything else that might indicate an injury or health concern.

In between these yearly examinations, if you notice anything that makes you suspect that your Golden Retriever isn't completely healthy, you should consult with your veterinarian immediately. An alert dog owner can help the veterinarian keep a dog healthy by noticing early signs of illness and seeking medical help before problems become worse. Some early signs of illness include the following:

- changes in energy or activity level
- changes in elimination habits or appetite, and amount of water consumed
- uncharacteristic moodiness, grumpiness, or sensitivity to touch or sound.

These kinds of changes don't necessarily mean that your dog is sick, but they might, especially if you observe several suspicious signs within the same week.

Many illnesses are preventable with healthy feeding, proper exercise, and good general care. There are some health issues, however, that a dog can be born with or be predisposed to through heredity. Before breeding, responsible dog breeders have all their animals tested for any inheritable abnormalities to which the breed is prone. Here are some disorders and diseases that appear fairly commonly in Golden Retrievers.

Hip and Elbow Dysplasia: These structural abnormalities of the hip and elbow are found in many, if not most, large breeds, including the Golden Retriever. Hip dysplasia is a malformation of the hip socket and/or the head of the femur (the thigh bone). Elbow dysplasia results

Normal internal temperature for a dog is between 100.2° and 102.8° Fahrenheit (38° and 39° Celsius).

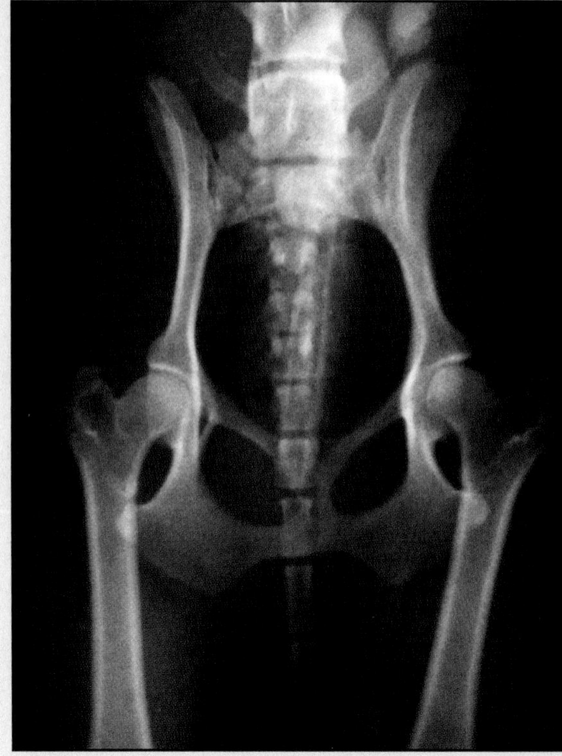

This x-ray shows the hip bone malformation that causes hip dysplasia in Golden Retrievers.

when a small bone in the elbow fails to fuse properly during puppyhood. Both abnormalities can be crippling and painful or just uncomfortable, depending on how much the bone is deformed and whether bone rubs against bone whenever the dog moves. In many cases surgery can relieve the pain and lameness that result from hip and elbow dysplasia, allowing the dog to live a more normal life.

Dysplasia is hereditary, but can be made worse or better, depending on the care given to the growing pup. Overfeeding and excessive exercise can both worsen these conditions, so it's best to keep pups on the lean side and be sensible about exercise.

Responsible breeders always x-ray their dogs' hips and elbows before they decide whether to breed them. The x-rays are sent to the Orthopedic Foundation for Animals for evaluation, and the dog's owner can use the results to decide whether her dog is sound enough to breed. As the practice of x-raying dogs for dysplasia before breeding them has grown more common, the incidence of these disorders has begun to diminish. However, because of the complex genetic blueprint for dysplasia, it's unlikely that x-ray evaluation of breeding stock will ever completely eradicate these disorders.

Bloat and Torsion: The technical name for bloat with torsion is gastric-dilatation volvulus (GDV). This condition occurs most frequently

Bad breath in dogs originates more often in the stomach than in the mouth.

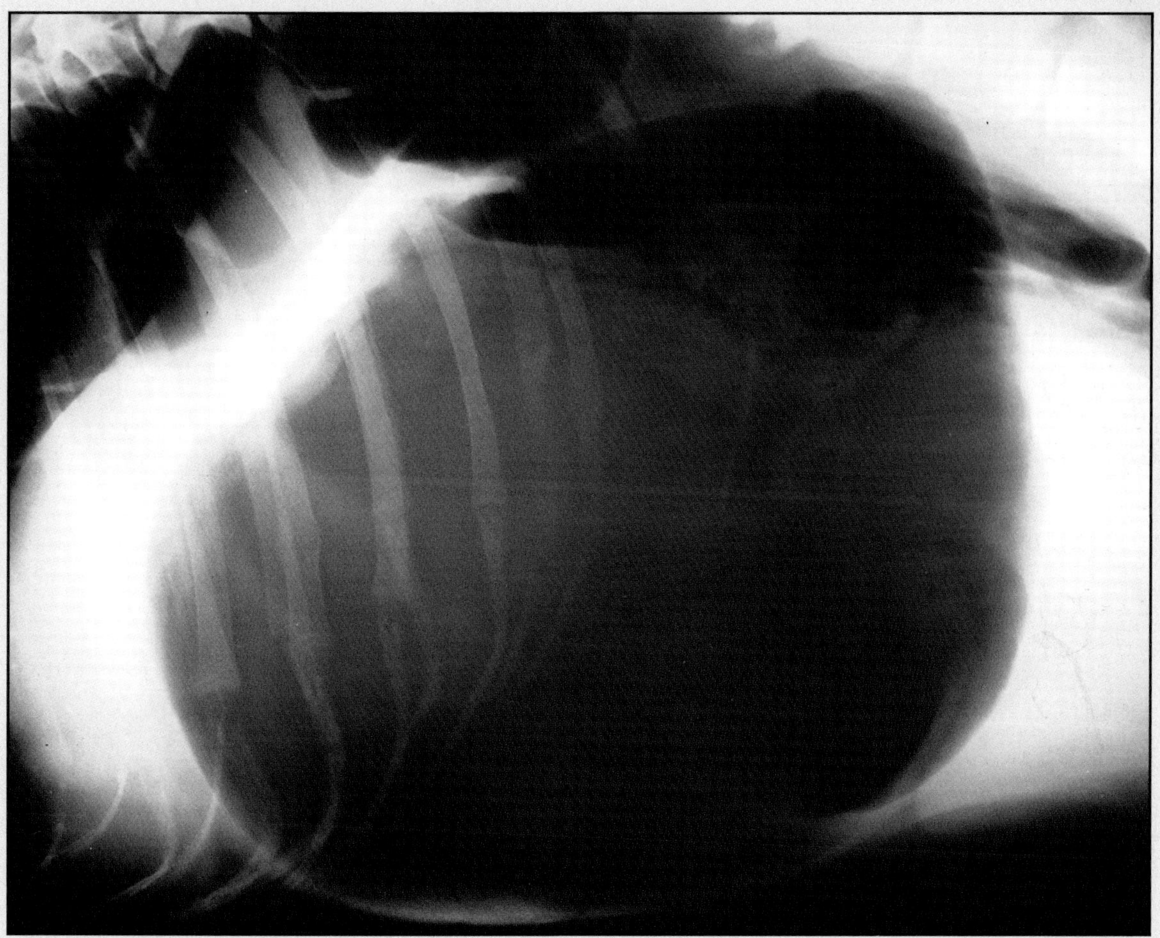

Bloat is a potentially fatal condition that affects large breeds like Golden Retrievers. The dark area in this x-ray of a dog's stomach shows the gas trapped inside.

in deep-chested dogs over 40 pounds (18 kg). The Golden Retriever is one breed that runs a higher-than-average risk for bloat and torsion.

Bloat involves the rapid formation and buildup of large quantities of gas and foamy mucus in the stomach. Bloat has a sudden and unpredictable onset and progresses rapidly. The pressure of the gas causes the stomach to expand inside the abdominal cavity and press against the heart, lungs, and abdominal blood vessels. The bloated stomach impinging on internal organs restricts their function and creates a painful and terrifying situation for the dog. Bloat can quickly become a life-threatening emergency, particularly if it's accompanied by torsion.

Torsion is a rotation of the stomach that pinches off its entrance from the esophagus and its exit through the duodenum. This traps water, food, gas, and foam, causing the stomach to swell even more. The blood builds up carbon dioxide because the inner abdominal pressure prevents the heart and lungs from doing their jobs of cleansing and oxygenating the blood. The dog's blood pressure drops, his body becomes toxic, and the stomach continues to become painfully distended.

The effects of bloat and torsion can kill a dog in under an hour. Bloat is an emergency that requires immediate veterinary intervention. If you think your dog is having an episode of bloat, head for the veterinary hospital right away. Call before leaving home and let the veterinarian know that you're on your way with a dog suffering from bloat. Then load your dog in the car and drive! Don't dawdle; the veterinarian may need those precious minutes to perform emergency surgery to save your dog's life.

The most common male dog names are Max, Jake, Buddy, Bailey, and Sam. The most common female dog names are Maggie, Molly, Lady, Sadie, and Lucy.

For several decades it was widely believed that elevating food and water bowls to the dog's chest height would help prevent bloat. However, a study by veterinarians at Purdue University showed that elevating the food bowl nearly doubles the likelihood of bloat.

When a dog comes in with bloat, the veterinarian will attempt to relieve the pressure by passing a large tube into the stomach by way of the mouth. If there is torsion, the tube will not get past that blockage. In this case, the only way to save the dog is to make an incision through the abdomen and into the stomach so the gas can escape.

Once the pressure is relieved, the veterinarian can reposition the stomach. Dogs that bloat once will usually bloat again. To prevent torsion, the veterinarian will "tack" the stomach to the muscles around the ribs, using surgical sutures, so the stomach cannot twist out of position if the dog bloats again.

The causes of bloat are not yet known for certain, though there seems to be a hereditary predisposition for it in certain dogs, and a number of possible environmental and situational triggers. Gulping air while eating may be one cause, so feed him two smaller meals a day instead of one big meal. It's easier for your Golden to thoroughly digest his food when there is less food in his stomach. Also, soak your Golden Retriever's kibble in warm water before you feed it to him. This will cause the kibble to expand before it gets into his stomach. Keeping your Golden Retriever calm and content after he eats helps prevent bloat, so don't let him exercise or play vigorously for at least an hour after meals.

Several antacid remedies made for human use contain an ingredient called simethicone, which can help slow or reduce the gas building up in a dog's stomach during a bloat episode. Always keep one of those products in your dog's first-aid kit, so it's accessible immediately if your dog starts to bloat. It can be given to a Golden Retriever in the same dosage as recommended for people. If you can slow down the expansion of gas in your dog's stomach, it may mean less pain for your dog and it will slow the dangerous progression of bloat into torsion.

Von Willebrand's Disease: This is the most common hereditary bleeding disorder found in dogs. It has been diagnosed in over fifty breeds, and the Golden Retriever is one with a higher-than-average incidence. This disease is caused by a deficiency of a plasma protein necessary for proper clotting of the blood, which results in prolonged internal bleeding. The condition is diagnosable with a blood test. It cannot be cured, although your veterinarian can treat excessive bleeding with special hormones or blood-clotting medicines. Golden Retrievers should be tested and found clear of Von Willebrand's disease before being used for breeding.

Eye Disorders: Hereditary cataracts are a common eye problem in Golden Retrievers. A cataract is a form of opacity within the lens of the eye. Some types of hereditary cataracts appear in fairly young adult Goldens. Some cataracts interfere with the dog's vision only slightly, but others may progress into severe or total vision loss. Nonhereditary cataracts may also occur in Goldens. A board-certified veterinary ophthalmologist can determine if the cataract is of concern from a genetic standpoint. If the cataract is suspected to be an inheritable type, the dog should not be used for breeding.

Some Goldens carry genes for progressive retinal atrophy (PRA), a hereditary condition that progressively destroys the dog's retina. Eventually, this condition will lead to total blindness. A noticeable loss of vision without evidence of cataracts is a good indication that a dog may have PRA. There is no treatment for this condition.

Golden Retrievers can also develop eyelid deformities, some of which are hereditary. Entropion is a turning inward of the eyelids; ectropion is the opposite, with the eyelids turning outward. Either condition can cause severe irritation to the eye. Surgery can correct these problems, but affected dogs should not be bred and, under AKC rules, are ineligible to be shown in Conformation competitions. They may compete in Obedience, Agility, and other events, though.

NUTRITION FOR THE ADULT DOG

Though most adult dogs could get by with only one daily meal, dogs are more comfortable being fed twice a day. Dividing your dog's daily ration into two smaller meals will help keep him from feeling overly hungry. Also, two smaller meals mean that he'll have less in his stomach at any one time, which reduces the likelihood of bloat.

Adult Golden Retrievers need a balanced diet with high-quality protein to build and repair muscles, skin, organs, and blood. Dogs use the fat in their diet as a main source of energy, so the quality and quantity of fat in their food is important. Too much fat can cause loose stools and also tax the digestive system, especially the pancreas, yet too little fat is not healthy either. Kibble diets are generally high in carbohydrates from grains or potatoes. These carbohydrates can be used by the dog for energy but are not generally as digestible for that purpose as fats.

A healthy diet must be readily digestible, nutritionally balanced, and fed in the correct amount for the individual dog. Dogs gain weight if they consume more food than they need for exercise and body maintenance.

Between meals, your Golden will enjoy treats he can chew, like this rawhide bone.

TOO FAT?

Most Golden Retrievers are very fond of eating and will happily consume more calories every day than they burn. Dogs of this breed are designed to work hard and get hours of exercise every day to turn their food into energy and muscle. If a Golden sits around all week instead, yet eats the same amount he'd need if he were working, he'll start packing on the pounds. Though a tendency toward overweight is very common in this breed, that excess weight is not healthy. Many Goldens will get pudgy in puppyhood, grow chubbier during adolescence, and then head toward full-fledged obesity once they reach their adult growth.

If your Golden Retriever is healthy and energetic but you can't feel his ribs without a little poking and prodding, he's probably fatter than he should be. Cut back a little on the size of his meals and add a bit more exercise to his daily routine. Don't make sudden radical changes in his food or activity level; these could put stress on your Golden Retriever and compromise his health. Gradual, steady steps toward reaching his optimum weight are healthier for your dog, and it is easier to keep weight off when it is lost gradually.

If you cannot feel your Golden Retriever's ribs at all, he may be seriously overweight. Obesity is a medical issue that can lead to problems with the heart and other vital systems. Make an appointment to have your veterinarian examine him and determine how best to change his diet and exercise regimen. Don't put this off. Obesity can seriously shorten a dog's life span.

They lose weight if they burn more calories than they get from the food they're eating. This seems so simple, but many dog owners don't realize the importance of observing their dog's weight and adjusting his food intake accordingly. Few responsible dog owners would underfeed their dogs to unhealthy thinness, but many overfeed them to a state of morbid obesity. Extra pounds on a dog steal years from his life, so don't let your Golden Retriever become obese.

It's easy to determine if your dog is maintaining a healthy weight. Stand him up and look down at his back from above. You should be able to see a waist between your dog's last set of ribs and his hips. If there's little or no waistline, the dog is overweight. If you can see hip and spine bones clearly outlined through the fur, your dog is too thin.

Dogs that are obese often suffer from musculoskeletal problems, diabetes, respiratory diseases, and many other health problems.

Now look at your standing dog from the side. There should be a bit of a tuck-up to the lower abdomen, just ahead of the rear legs. If there's little or no tuck-up there, the dog is overweight. If you can see the curve of every rib through the fur, the dog is too thin.

Now feel your dog's side with the tips of your fingers. You should be able to count his ribs without having to dig for them. If you can feel each rib with your fingertips, he's lean enough. Then run your flat palm along your dog's side. If it feels firm and smooth, then he has enough flesh and muscle. If you feel every rib against your hand, the dog is too thin.

When it comes to health, a lean body in a dog is generally preferable to a fat one. Numerous scientifically controlled experiments have proven that lean animals tend to have fewer chronic health problems and tend to live longer than overweight individuals of the same species. For example, one fourteen-year study published in the May 2002 issue of the *Journal of the American Veterinary Medical Association* found that lean dogs lived an average of 15 percent—nearly two years—longer than the control animals in the study.

EXERCISE

An adult Golden Retriever needs daily exercise to stay healthy and keep his mood upbeat and positive. A shortage of regular exercise leads to weakened muscles, including the heart. Insufficient exercise can also make a dog restless and irritable, which can contribute to behavior problems, like excessive barking or destructive chewing.

Exercise should be provided daily: this builds stamina and conditions the muscles without overtaxing the dog's current strength or endurance. It's not healthy for your Golden Retriever to sit idle all week, then exercise to exhaustion on the weekend. That all-or-nothing weekend-athlete approach to exercise can cause strains, sprains, and other injuries that may be slow to heal.

For good conditioning, nothing beats free-running play on soft ground with other dogs. This isn't always practical or possible, though, so it's important to provide some

Your Golden Retriever requires regular exercise in order to stay healthy and happy.

other exercise that gives your Golden Retriever a good aerobic workout and uses all his muscles. To stay fit and prevent flab, your Golden Retriever needs a daily minimum of two brisk one-mile (1.6 km) walks, plus at least a half-hour of vigorous off-leash exercise like swimming, fetching, or running with dog pals. For continuing good health, your dog needs at least this much daily exercise, and more would be even better.

ADVANCED TRAINING

If you enjoyed teaching your pup the basics, you'll probably enjoy teaching him advanced skills even more.

Conformation: Conformation shows are competitive events where Golden Retrievers and purebred dogs of other breeds are judged against the written Standard of Perfection for their breed. The standard describes the ideal appearance, gait, and temperament of the breed. Males and females are judged separately, and the winner in each sex is awarded from one to five championship points. The number of points is determined by how many dogs competed. Winners in both sexes are then judged together, along with Champions, and one dog among them is selected as the Best of Breed (BOB) for that day.

To succeed, a show dog must adhere closely to the physical requirements of the breed standard. If your Golden Retriever has a great personality, that may also help his chances in a Conformation event.

The Best of Breed winner goes on to compete with the other BOB winners from his breed's group. Golden Retrievers are in the Sporting Group. The other six groups are Hound, Working, Terrier, Toy, Non-Sporting, and Herding. The winners from each of the groups compete together for Best in Show.

A Conformation dog must be kept in the peak of health in order to win. Your Golden Retriever's muscles should be well developed and firm, his eyes should be bright and clear, his coat should shine. Conformation dogs are trained to trot so the judge can see how they move ("gait") and pose for presentation and examination by the judge ("stack").

A show dog must allow himself to be handled all over by a stranger (the judge), including the mouth, the teeth, and, for males, the testicles. In the conformation ring, the judge evaluates both temperament and physique for conformance to the Standard of Perfection.

Obedience: Obedience trials may be held in conjunction with Conformation shows or as standalone events. Obedience trials test a dog's response to his handler. The dog must obey verbal commands and hand signals immediately, precisely, and willingly. The handler is allowed to command the dog once, and then must give no further cues until the exercise is finished. Between exercises, the handler is allowed to praise and pet the dog, but the dog must remain under control.

There are several levels of difficulty in Obedience, with a title to be earned at each level by attaining three to ten qualifying scores at that level. A qualifying score in Obedience is 170 or better. A perfect score is 200.

Novice Obedience requires the dog to heel close to his handler's left side, both on-leash and off-leash, as they walk, turn, halt, and change speeds as directed by the judge. The dog must stay when told, then come when called and sit facing the handler within easy reach. Each dog must do an individual stand-stay, allowing the judge to touch him, and then they all perform sit and down stays together, for one and three minutes, respectively. Three qualifying scores at the Novice level earn the Companion Dog (CD) title.

The next level is Open, where the dogs heel a pattern off-leash as the judge directs. There are jumps and retrieving exercises in Open, and for the group sit and down stays, the handlers must leave their dogs and wait out of sight for three and five minutes, respectively. Three qualifying scores in Open earn the Companion Dog Excellent (CDX) title.

The next advanced level in Obedience is called Utility. Here the handler does a silent signal exercise, cueing the dog to sit, down, stand, stay, and come, using only hand signals. There is a send-out, where the dog must run to the far end of the ring, turn, and sit facing the handler, waiting to be signaled which of two

In the early 1970s, the American Kennel Club first started offering Obedience Trial Championship (OTCH) titles. The first three dogs to earn the OTCH title were all Golden Retrievers.

jumps he must leap on the way back in. In a directed retrieve in Utility, the judge designates which of three cotton work gloves the handler will send the dog to fetch.

Utility also calls for a scent discrimination exercise. This requires matching sets of five metal articles and five leather articles. These can be dumbbell-shaped articles manufactured for Obedience training or common objects made of those materials, in sets of five identical items. (For example, five identical leather moccasins and five identical metal tablespoons may be used.) The objects are placed on the floor at the other end of the ring, after the handler holds one for a few moments to scent it. On the judge's signal, the handler sends the dog to find the scented item. The dog sniffs the pile of objects and retrieves the correct one. An item of the other material is then scented by the handler and placed among the remaining articles. The dog must find that second scented item and carry it to the handler.

Three qualifying scores in Utility earn a competitor the Utility Dog (UD) title. Dogs can earn the Utility Dog Excellent (UDX) title by earning qualifying scores in both Open and Utility classes at the same trial, and by doing that ten times.

Rally: In this sport the dog and handler heel together around a course of numbered stations, each with a sign indicating an exercise for the handler and the dog to perform. Each of more than fifty exercises tests the dog and handler's teamwork skills. In Rally the handler is permitted to talk to and encourage the dog as much as she wants. The handler is allowed to praise the dog, but not pet him, both while performing the exercises and when moving between them.

Novice-level Rally is performed on-leash. Advanced and Excellent Rally levels are performed off-leash. A perfect score in AKC Rally is 100. Titles are earned at each level with three qualifying scores of 70 or higher. The titles are Rally Novice (RN), Rally Advanced (RA), and Rally Excellent (RE). Another title, the Rally Advanced Excellent (RAE), can be earned after completing the RE. This additional title requires the team to earn qualifying scores in both Advanced and Excellent classes at the same trial, and to do that ten times.

Some Rally exercises are similar to Obedience exercises—sits, downs, stays, call-fronts, finishes-to-heel, stands, and figure-8s. There are also challenging exercises not used in Obedience, with heeling through serpentines and elongated spirals. There

THE COSTS OF COMPETITION

If you decide to get involved in competitive sports with your Golden Retriever, the annual cost of owning your dog will skyrocket, as you add on the following expenses:

Entry fees: $20 to $30 for each class entered. Depending on which sports and how many you compete in with your dog, entry fees for one show or trial can run from $20 to $100, or more.

Transportation: Fuel for your car or motor home to drive to shows within driving distance, and plane fare for important shows farther from home, such as the Golden Retriever Club of America's annual National Specialty show.

Lodging: Hotel or motel rooms range from $80 to several hundred dollars a night, depending on quality, location, and whether or not the pet fee charged by the hotel is refundable. At some events, participants are permitted to camp on the show grounds. If you own a motor home or camping trailer, this option usually costs from $15 to $50 a night.

Meals away from home: Budget appropriately, depending on your appetite and tastes as well as where you're going.

Handler's fees: $100 to $600 or more per show. Hiring a professional handler to exhibit your Golden Retriever in Conformation, instead of handling him yourself, can increase your dog's success in the show ring, but the cost of earning those awards will increase as well.

Photographs of wins: When your Golden wins at a show, captures a title, or earns a perfect score, you will want to get a photograph to remember the day. Sponsoring clubs arrange to have one or more professional photographers on site at the show to provide that service to exhibitors. Dog show photographers generally charge between $25 and $35 per print.

are many different turns in Rally, including 90-degree and 180-degree turns, as encountered in Obedience, and 270-degree and 360-degree turns to both left and right.

In Rally, the judge only tells the team when to start. From then on, the handler guides herself and her dog around the ring, following the course without direction from the judge. The team moves from sign to sign in numbered order, performing each one as described in the regulations.

Gentleness on the part of the handler and willingness on the part of the dog are hallmarks of an exemplary Rally team. Everything a dog and handler do from the moment they enter the Rally ring gate until they leave the ring after their run affects their score. Handler mistakes—such as guiding the dog with a tight leash, making collar-jerk corrections, or speaking sharply to the dog—or dog mistakes, like being uncooperative getting into start position, can lose points for the team before they even start the course.

When the handler and dog are at the start sign, the judge asks, "Are you ready?" The handler checks her dog to be sure he's in position beside her, and then replies to the judge, "Yes," or "Ready." The judge then says, "Forward," and, from there on, says nothing more. The judge silently follows behind or to the side of the team at a distance and angle that provides the best view of each station. The judge scores the team's performance as they proceed from sign to sign, doing each exercise along the course.

The handler may speak to and encourage the dog as much as she wants. Repeated cues and signals are not penalized, and if the team cannot successfully perform an exercise on their first attempt, a retry is allowed. The retry costs the team three points off their final score, but if the retry is successful, that three-point deduction is less "expensive" than losing a full ten points for incorrectly performing the station.

Agility: This sport is judged on speed and accuracy over a course of jumps, tunnels, ramps, and other obstacles. Each dog is timed as he individually races over a numbered obstacle course, as directed by his handler. In Agility, the dog performs the jumps and obstacles and the handler does not. The handler may run with the dog, directing him from up close, or may direct him from behind, front, or side at a greater distance.

The experienced Agility dog learns to respond instantly on the course to subtle movements of his handler's shoulders, hips, and knees as cues for changes in direction or pace. Most handlers also use hand signals and verbal cues to give their dogs specific information, like which one of two side-by-side obstacles to tackle. Handlers may also talk, clap, praise, and verbally encourage the dog, but may not touch the dog or any of the obstacles.

In Agility, a dog can earn titles at the Novice, Open, and Advanced levels by earning three qualifying scores for each level. First-place through fourth-place ribbons are awarded to

A Golden Retriever jumps an obstacle as part of the Agility competition.

the dogs with the fewest faults and the fastest run times. Dogs compete for placements only against other dogs of their same approximate height. A dog can earn titles without placing.

All the jumps on a course are set at a height appropriate for each competitor. Tall dogs have higher jumps than short dogs, which helps make Agility fair for all. To determine the proper jump height division for the dog, a judge at an Agility trial will measure him at the withers and issue a height card with the dog's official measurement. Jumps are adjusted from four inches (10 cm) high to 24 inches (61 cm) or more. Golden Retrievers typically must clear heights of 16, 20, or 24 inches (40.5, 51, or 61 cm) in Agility. Only the jumps are adjusted for the dogs' height; the other obstacles stay the same for all dogs.

AKC Agility classes include Standard, in which the contestants cover a course that uses all possible obstacles, and Jumpers with Weaves, in which the course only includes jumps and weave poles. There is now also a challenging course, the FAST class, where the dog is directed over part of the course by the handler from a distance. Other organizations offer Agility contests similar to those sanctioned by the American Kennel Club, as well as contests that are different.

ASSISTANCE DOGS

Golden Retrievers have proven their merit in the assistance dog work world as well as in sports. Goldens make reliable service dogs, helping people with physical or emotional disabilities to do things they cannot do without help. A well-trained service dog can do most of the tasks that would otherwise necessitate hiring a human helper. The dogs carry groceries, retrieve dropped or distant items, pull wheelchairs, help the person in and out of bed, help the person dress and undress, fetch drinks from the fridge, open and close heavy doors, help with laundry, make beds, and perform many other helpful tasks.

Golden Retrievers have long served as guides to the blind. A guide dog learns to recognize and avoid situations that might endanger his blind partner. Normally, when the person commands the dog to move forward, that's what the dog will immediately do. However, if the dog is commanded to do anything that endangers his partner, he will refuse to move.

Golden Retrievers can also serve as hearing assistance dogs. These dogs are trained to alert their deaf or hearing-impaired human partner to important sounds, like the person's name, a baby's cry, an alarm clock's ring, the oven timer's buzz, and the fire alarm's wail. When the dog hears the sound, he goes to the person and gives a signal, such as a nudge with his nose, indicating that he has heard something the person needs to know about. Once the hearing dog gets the person's attention, he will indicate the source of the sound, so the person can respond to it properly.

THERAPY DOGS

Golden Retrievers typically enjoy people and appreciate attention, even from strangers. They seem to know just how to give comfort to someone who needs it. Many Goldens participate in pet-assisted therapy, visiting nursing homes and other care facilities to bring residents the joy and unconditional affection only a dog can give.

Some Golden Retrievers serve as emotional therapy dogs, too, helping patients open up to

Golden Retrievers make excellent service dogs. This dog is being trained to become a guide dog. The training, which began when he was a puppy, enables him to serve as his master's "eyes."

Because of their gentle and friendly nature, Golden Retrievers make wonderful therapy dogs.

something outside themselves and begin to heal. Emotionally traumatized individuals who have become unable to speak or relate to human beings often find comfort and safety in the nonjudgmental affection of a large, gentle, sweet Golden Retriever.

SEARCH-AND-RESCUE DOGS

The Golden Retriever is athletic and agile, has a great nose, and generally likes people and gets along with other dogs. This suits them well for search-and-rescue (SAR) training.

SAR dogs must not be aggressive toward people or other dogs, since they'll need to work cooperatively in group search settings. They must be able to ignore fresh deer and rabbit trails that cross the faint scent of the lost hiker whose trail they're following. They must be courageous enough to ride in open boats, helicopters, snowplows, ski lifts, and any other conveyance that can take a SAR team where the missing person may have left a scent.

A SAR dog is trained to do what comes naturally—follow his nose—and his nose can lead his handler to the person whose scent he has been asked to track. The SAR dog can find items the size of a match that the person had handled and dropped weeks earlier in the middle of a hundred-acre field. That's not even particularly difficult for a trained dog.

SAR work requires dogs and their handlers to be strong, fit, and able to work long hours with little rest, night or day, in freezing storms or blazing heat. The only pay the handlers receive is the satisfaction of having helped someone. And Golden Retrievers are also satisfied with that kind of pay.

Following the September 11, 2001, terrorist attacks on the World Trade Center in New York, Golden Retrievers were prominent among the search-and-rescue dogs searching for survivors.

CANINE GOOD CITIZEN

The American Kennel Club's Canine Good Citizen (CGC) Test is open to dogs of all breeds, as well as mixes. This CGC Test involves ten exercises that test the dog's social and obedience skills. He must walk on-leash without pulling; sit, lie down, and walk through a crowd; ignore a dog that is close by; stay where told and come when called; let strangers pet him, groom him, and hold him while his owner leaves

No matter how highly trained your adult Golden Retriever is, he'll always be interested in spending time outdoors—preferably with you.

the room for several minutes; withstand sudden loud noises or visual stimulation without overreacting; and show his ability to perform a few other real-life skills.

Dogs that pass the CGC Test are issued certificates touting that achievement. The benefits of CGC certification go beyond the obvious one of having a well-behaved dog. Some homeowner's insurance companies require CGC certification before they insure owners of certain breeds. Some communities are considering lowering the license fees for dogs that have earned CGC certificates, and some landlords will reduce, or even waive, their standard pet deposit for CGC dogs.

TEMPERAMENT TEST

Temperament Evaluation Tests are held by local and regional dog clubs around the United States. Any breed or mix can take the test. At these events, a trained evaluator observes each dog in turn as he goes through a series of structured exercises. The exercises present specific situations, such as a friendly stranger, a threatening stranger, the startling opening of an umbrella, the sound of gunfire, and additional sounds and situations.

The evaluator scores the dog on courage, protectiveness, and other qualities of temperament. Those dogs that pass receive a certificate and are permitted to add the initials TT (Temperament Tested) after their name, to signify their achievement. If the dog doesn't pass the test the first time, he can be retested later.

CHAPTER EIGHT

Caring for Your Senior Dog

Golden Retrievers become seniors at around ten to twelve years old. As your Golden ages, his body will go through gradual changes, both externally and internally. His digestive system will slow

As your Golden ages, he will begin to grey around the face and muzzle.

down and becomes less efficient, and his metabolism may slow down as well. The heart muscle gradually weakens, as do other muscles throughout the body. Tumors, cysts, and other growths may appear. His hearing may fade and his eyesight may dim. Cancer, heart disease, diabetes, stroke, nervous system disorders, and other age-related health problems plague senior dogs, just as they do older humans.

There are no cures for aging, but there are ways to make your Golden Retriever's senior years more comfortable.

WATCHING FOR CANCER

There are many types of cancer, and some are more deadly than others. Cancer seems to strike randomly; it is difficult to predict and its causes are not always understood. Certain cancers are hereditary, but variables such as diet and stress can raise or lower an individual's risk.

The best way to detect cancer early is to be alert to any changes in your dog's body or health that might indicate that something is not right. As you pet your Golden Retriever, let your fingers wander over his body. Lumps, bumps, and slow-to-heal sores can sometimes indicate cancer. If you feel something unusual, take a closer look and keep an eye on that spot for a week. Any sores, given proper cleaning and care, that don't heal within a week, or any lumps that don't go away in that time, should be checked by the veterinarian.

Bad breath can originate from dirty teeth, but it can also indicate internal health problems, including cancer. A sudden case of foul breath often signals simple indigestion, but if your Golden Retriever's breath usually smells bad, have the veterinarian examine him. If the doctor suspects anything beyond indigestion, she may suggest blood and/or urine tests to screen for more serious health problems, including cancer.

Different cancers are treated with different types of medical intervention. Treatment may include surgical

Due to better diets, better living conditions, and advances in veterinary medicine, dogs are living longer than ever. Pet-product manufacturers are paying attention to the aging pet population. Supplements, special diets, low-calorie treats, and an abundance of health products and devices to comfort aging pets are now widely available at pet supply outlets.

removal of tumors, radiation, and chemotherapy. Dietary supplements may be prescribed to strengthen general health both during and after other treatments. Some types of cancers, when detected early, have a good prognosis for successful treatment and recovery.

INCONTINENCE

Dogs in their senior years sometimes lose control over their bladder and bowels. Medications can help in some cases, but not all. Be diligent about keeping your incontinent dog clean. Wash and thoroughly dry him when he wets himself, so his skin doesn't become scalded by leaked urine. You will also need to change his bedding every time he soils it. To cut down on laundry, you can have your incontinent Golden wear a dog diaper with disposable absorbent pads. There are waterproof belly-bands for male dogs and panties designed for females in sizes to fit Golden Retrievers. The absorbent pads must be changed whenever they become soiled.

Most incontinent senior dogs are aware that they are soiling themselves, their bed, and your floor. A senior Golden Retriever who has been clean since he was a puppy may become frustrated and ashamed because of his incontinence. Try to disguise your own frustration with your dog's lack of bladder or bowel control, and never punish your incontinent dog for something beyond his control.

You can't always prevent or cure age-related conditions, but you can improve your Golden's quality of life by keeping him as comfortable as possible. Don't forget to investigate alternative therapies, such as acupuncture, chiropractic, herbal remedies, homeopathic remedies, aromatherapy, Tellington Touch, massage, or other health options.

NUTRITION

As a dog ages, his digestive system often becomes less efficient, making it more important than ever for the food he consumes to be high quality and easily digested. Most senior dogs exercise less than when they were younger, so it's generally advisable to reduce the senior dog's caloric intake to prevent excessive weight gain.

An elderly dog in good health can usually maintain proper weight on the same food he has always eaten, but the serving size must be reduced to match his lower metabolism and activity level. Some senior dogs

A dog that is 15 percent over his desirable weight is susceptible to obesity-related health problems.

develop problems with their metabolism, though. If that occurs, it may not be enough to simply change the size of his portions. Ask your veterinarian to help develop a diet that will keep your Golden in the best condition through his senior years.

If your aging Golden has heart, liver, or kidney problems, he may need a special diet. Various prescription diets, available from veterinarians, are formulated specifically to help a dog stay as healthy as possible despite impaired organ function. If your dog needs some of these specialized rations, your veterinarian can prescribe the right one.

EXERCISE

Your senior Golden still needs regular daily exercise to keep his heart, lungs, bones, and muscles healthy

Swimming is a fantastic way to keep your older Golden in good shape. Swimming is easy on the joints but still gives him the cardiopulmonary workout he needs.

Older dogs are more susceptible to the effects of temperature extremes, so don't leave your elderly Golden Retriever outside when it's extremely hot or cold, and watch your dog for signs of temperature-related distress.

and working properly. Lack of exercise will cause muscles, including the heart muscle, to atrophy. An inactive Golden will likely become overweight. The combination of overweight and physical weakness will lead to a downward spiral of inactivity, further weakness, and worsening health.

You can help your Golden slow down age-related deterioration by keeping him active as he ages. Obviously, this does not mean taking your 12-year-old Golden Retriever mountain climbing or swimming in whitewater rapids, even if he did these activities easily in his younger days. Few senior humans can safely revisit the extreme sports of their youth, and neither can most senior dogs. However, moderate daily exercise will help your Golden stay healthy and active for years.

Make a point of giving your senior Golden a daily walk or play a few rounds of fetch with him. Let him set the pace for these activities, and be willing, as he ages, to allow those walks and games to become slower.

OLD AGE AND SAYING GOOD-BYE

Nothing lasts forever, at least nothing mortal. Eventually the time will come when you and your beloved elderly Golden Retriever must say good-bye to each other. This will be a sad and reflective time, as you page back through your memories and recall all the good times that you two had together. Your Golden is not alone in his aging—you have aged too, though his dog years have aged him faster than your human years.

When you realize that your Golden Retriever's time to leave is

After your pet passes away, you'll have to make final arrangements. The most common methods of laying a pet to rest are cremation and full body burial. Most veterinarians offer cremation services and pet cemetery recommendations. If your vet doesn't, you can locate a private crematorium or pet cemetery through the Web site of the International Association of Pet Cemeteries and Crematories, www.iaopc.com.

It is very rare for a dog to die peacefully of old age in his sleep. If your dog is in extreme pain from a debilitating or terminal disease, and can no longer enjoy even the simplest pleasures, it may be time to consider euthanasia.

getting close, there are some things you can do to help ease this final transition for both of you.

Take some new photographs of your Golden. If possible, revisit some of the places that hold good memories of sweet times and earlier adventures with your dog, and have a friend photograph you and your Golden there.

As the time approaches to say good-bye, put your feelings on paper, in a journal or notebook. You might simply jot down thoughts as they occur to you, or you might find the words to put them into poetry. Either way, journaling can help release some of the emotions you will probably feel at this difficult and emotional time.

Pick a special place to bury your Golden's remains or to scatter his ashes after he's gone. Take your dog there and share a picnic or just sit and pet him, if he feels well enough to enjoy an outing. That way the spot will hold recent memories of a pleasant time together.

Saying good-bye to your best friend will not be easy. Take some photographs of you and your dog together. Reviewing them after his passing will help you grieve.

Other people who love your Golden Retriever deserve an opportunity to say good-bye to him as well. If your dog has made many friends in his life, invite over some of those special people who care deeply for both of you, and give them and your Golden the chance to see each other again. Photograph or videotape that sharing time if you can; it will be a treasure for you later.

Your Golden may pass away quietly in his sleep, or he may cling to life stubbornly, even as his physical systems are shutting down. As our dogs' best friends and caregivers, we have the option to provide a final kindness to our dogs: a painless passing.

Euthanasia—a term that means "good death"—is the planned killing of a dog by means of an injection. Your veterinarian will inject your dog with a cocktail of drugs that will put him to sleep. The initial poke aside, it's absolutely painless for your dog. Within a couple of minutes, your dog's heart will stop beating and he will be at rest. Of course, it will be very painful for you. Nobody wants to be forced to put a beloved animal companion to sleep. However, if keeping your precious Golden Retriever alive will only prolong his suffering, euthanasia may be the kindest thing you can do. If your Golden Retriever is suffering in his last days, talk over that option with your veterinarian and decide if it would be appropriate.

When you and your Golden Retriever do say your final good-bye for this lifetime, you can comfort yourself with knowing you've loved your old friend and provided for him in the best ways you could.

Organizations to Contact

American Animal Hospital Association
12575 West Bayaud Ave.
Lakewood, CO 80228
Phone: 303-986-2800
Fax: 800-252-2242
Email: info@aahanet.org
Web site: www.aahanet.org

American Kennel Club
260 Madison Ave
New York, NY 10016
Phone: 212-696-8200
Web site: www.akc.org

Association of Pet Dog Trainers
150 Executive Center Drive Box 35
Greenville, SC 29615
Phone: 800-738-3647
Fax: 864-331-0767
Email: information@apdt.com
Web site: www.apdt.com

The Canadian Kennel Club
89 Skyway Avenue, Suite 100
Etobicoke, Ontario
M9W 6R4 Canada
Phone: 416-675-5511
Fax: 416-675-6506
Email: information@ckc.ca
Web site: www.ckc.ca/en

Canine Eye Registration Foundation
1717 Philo Road
P.O. Box 3007
Urbana, IL 61803-3007
Phone: 217-693-4800
Fax: 217-693-4801
Email: cerf@vmdb.org
Web site: www.vmdb.org/cerf.html

Golden Retriever Breed Council
Email: webmaster@goldenretrievers.co.uk
Web site: www.goldenretrievers.co.uk

Golden Retriever Club of America
Barbara Branstad, secretary
6720 NCR 15
Fort Collins, CO 80524
Email: bbransta@lamar.colostate.edu
Web site: www.grca.org

Golden Retriever Club of Canada
Christine Kobler, secretary
P.O. Box 1286
Aldergrove BC V4W 2V1
Canada
Phone: 905-383-4380
Email: redgold@telus.net
Web site: www.grcc.net

Golden Retriever Club of the United Kingdom
Email: clivedonahue@aol.com
Web site:
www.thegoldenretrieverclub.co.uk

The Kennel Club of the United Kingdom
1-5 Clarges Street
Piccadilly
London W1J 8AB
United Kingdom
Phone: 0870 606 6750
Fax: 020 7518 1058
Web site: www.thekennelclub.org.uk

National Association of Dog Obedience Instructors
PMB 369
729 Grapevine Hwy
Hurst, TX 76054-2085
Email: corrsec2@nadoi.org
Web site: www.nadoi.org

National Association of Professional Pet Sitters
17000 Commerce Parkway, Suite C
Mt. Laurel, NJ 08054
Phone: 856-439-0324
Fax: 856-439-0525
Email: napps@ahint.com
Web site: www.petsitters.org

National Dog Registry
P.O. Box 51105
Mesa, AZ 85208
Phone: 800-NDR-DOGS
Email: info@nationaldogregistry.com
Web site:
www.nationaldogregistry.com

North American Dog Agility Council (NADAC)
11522 South Highway 3
Cataldo, ID 83810
Email: info@nadac.com
Web site: www.nadac.com

North American Flyball Association (NAFA)
1400 West Devon Avenue, #512
Chicago, IL 60660
Phone and fax: 800-318-6312
Email: flyball@flyball.org
Web site: www.flyball.org

Orthopedic Foundation for Animals (OFA)
2300 East Nifong Boulevard
Columbia, MO 65201-3806
Phone: 573-442-0418
Fax: 573-875-5073
Email: ofa@offa.org
Web site: www.offa.org

Pet Sitters International
418 East King Street
King, NC 27021-9163
Phone: 336-983-9222
Fax: 336-983-3755
Web site: www.petsit.com

Therapy Dogs International, Inc.
88 Bartley Road
Flanders, NJ 07836
Phone: 973-252-9800
Fax: 973-252-7171
Email: tdi@gti.net
Web site: www.tdi-dog.org

UK National Pet Register
74 North Albert Street, Dept 2
Fleetwood, Lancasterhire
FY7 6BJ
United Kingdom
Web site: www.nationalpetregister.org

United States Dog Agility Association, Inc. (USDAA)
P.O. Box 850955
Richardson, TX 75085-0955
Phone: 972-487-2200
Fax: 972-272-4404
Email: info@usdaa.com
Web site: www.usdaa.com

World Canine Freestyle Organization (WCFO)
P.O. Box 350122
Brooklyn, NY 11235-2525
Phone: 718-332-8336
Fax: 718-646-2686
Email: wcfodogs@aol.com
Web site: www.worldcaninefreestyle.org

Further Reading

Bauer, Nona Kilgore. *The World of the Golden Retriever: A Dog for All Seasons.* Neptune City, N.J.: TFH Publications, 1994.

Carlson, James, and Lisa Giffin. *Owner's Home Veterinary Handbook,* 3rd ed. New York: Howell Book House, 1999.

Charlesworth, W. M. *The Book of the Golden Retriever.* London: The Field, 1933.

Dennison, Pamela. *Click Your Way to Rally Obedience.* Loveland, Colo.: Alpine Publishing, 2006.

Foss, Valerie. *Ultimate Golden Retriever,* 2nd ed. New York: Howell Book House, 2003.

Green, Peter, and Mario Migliorini. *New Secrets of Successful Show Dog Handling*. Loveland, Colo.: Alpine Publishing, 2002.

Handler, Barbara. *Successful Obedience Handling,* 2nd ed. Loveland, Colo.: Alpine Publishing, 2003.

Koshar, Claire. *A Guide to Dog Sports.* Irvine, Calif.: Doral Publishing, 2002.

Pitcairn, Richard, and Susan Pitcairn. *Dr. Pitcairn's Complete Guide to Natural Health for Dogs and Cats,* 3rd ed. Emmaus, Pa.: Rodale Press, 2005.

Shojai, Amy. *First Aid Companion for Dogs and Cats.* Emmaus, Pa.: Rodale Press, 2001.

Internet Resources

www.adoa.org

The American Dog Owners Association is an organization devoted to responsible dog ownership and preserving the special relationship between dogs and humankind.

www.akc.org/breeds/golden_retriever

This page contains the American Kennel Club's description of the Golden Retriever breed standard.

www.ckc.ca/en/Default.aspx?tabid=99&BreedCode=RTG

This page contains the Canadian Kennel Club's description of the Golden Retriever breed standard.

www.clickersolutions.com

This Web site includes information and tips for training dogs and solving dog behavior problems without using force or strong aversives.

http://clickertraining.com

An educational resource with information and how-to tips about the modern, nonforce way of educating dogs through clicker training, a form of operant conditioning that is both effective and enjoyable.

Publisher's Note: The Web sites listed on these pages were active at the time of publication. The publisher is not responsible for Web sites that have changed their address or discontinued operation since the date of publication.

www.dogscouts.com

Dog Scouts of America is an organization that promotes responsible dog ownership through camps and other fun activities for dogs and their owners.

www.grca-nrc.org/Localrescues.htm

Information about Golden Retriever rescue volunteer groups, listed by state.

www.healthypet.com

The pet owner's Web site of the American Animal Hospital Association lists accredited veterinary hospitals in every state and provides up-to-date pet health information.

www.thekennelclub.org.uk/item/108

This page contains the Kennel Club of the United Kingdom's description of the Golden Retriever breed standard.

Index

Contributors

September Morn is a professional dog trainer and freelance writer, whose articles have appeared in *Dog Fancy, Popular Dogs, Dogs For Kids, Dogs USA, Puppies USA, Clean Run*, and *Your Dog*. Her previous books include *Training Your Labrador Retriever* (Barron's, 2000) and *Housetraining* (2nd ed., Howell/Wiley, 2006). September owns Dogs Love School, in Shelton, Washington, and currently shares her home and heart with three Rottweilers and two American Eskimo dogs.

Senior Consulting Editor **Gary Korsgaard, DVM,** has had a long and distinguished career in veterinary medicine. After graduating from The Ohio State University's College of Veterinary Medicine in 1963, he spent two years as a captain in the Veterinary Corps of the U.S. Army. During that time he attended the Walter Reed Army Institute of Research and became Chief of the Veterinary Division for the Sixth Army Medical Laboratory at the Presidio, San Francisco.

In 1968 Dr. Korsgaard founded the Monte Vista Veterinary Hospital in Concord, California, where he practiced for 32 years as a small animal veterinarian. He is a past president of the Contra Costa Veterinary Association, and was one of the founding members of the Contra Costa Veterinary Emergency Clinic, serving as president and board member of that hospital for nearly 30 years.

Dr. Korsgaard retired in 2000, and currently enjoys golf, hiking, international travel, and spending time with his wife Susan and their three children and four grandchildren.